Cobblestone Cats

Flamengo

Rio de Janeiro

Panattoni

Copyright ©2018 Alan Panattoni
All Rights Reserved

Published by:
Panattoni Press
P.O. BOX 9022381
SAN JUAN, PR 00902

www.panattoniprintshop.com

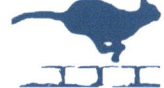

Cobblestone Cats

Cats of Flamengo

Although Rio was first settled by the French in 1555 the Portuguese first visited the region in 1502 and eventually took hold of the area after defeating the French in 1567. Today, Rio is Brazil's second largest metropolis, after Sao Paulo, with some 6.3 million inhabitants. It is an iconic ocean front city with fabulous sandy beaches, bikini fit men and woman, a plethora of modest football fields, and several public parks. One of these parks is Flamengo, located alongside Flamengo Beach just across the bay from tourist bound Sugarloaf Mountain. In this beautiful beach front park you will find locals biking, jogging, playing football in the sand, cross fitting, and of course cats.

Flamengo Park, also known as Aterro do Flamengo, which literally means "Landfill of Flamengo", is the largest leisure area in Rio de Janeiro and consist of nearly 300 acres. Throughout the acreage you will see dozens and dozens of cats with the majority of them being in good health. Most of the cats are friendly and will saunter up looking for a pat and cuddle. You will see them up in trees or cruising alongside the beach. The cats of Flamengo are looked after by dedicated locals who leave food and water for them through out the park, as well as, cushions for them to sleep on.

The Cats of Flamengo are documented through these pages....................

.... Enjoy!

An adult cat has 290 bones and 527 muscles

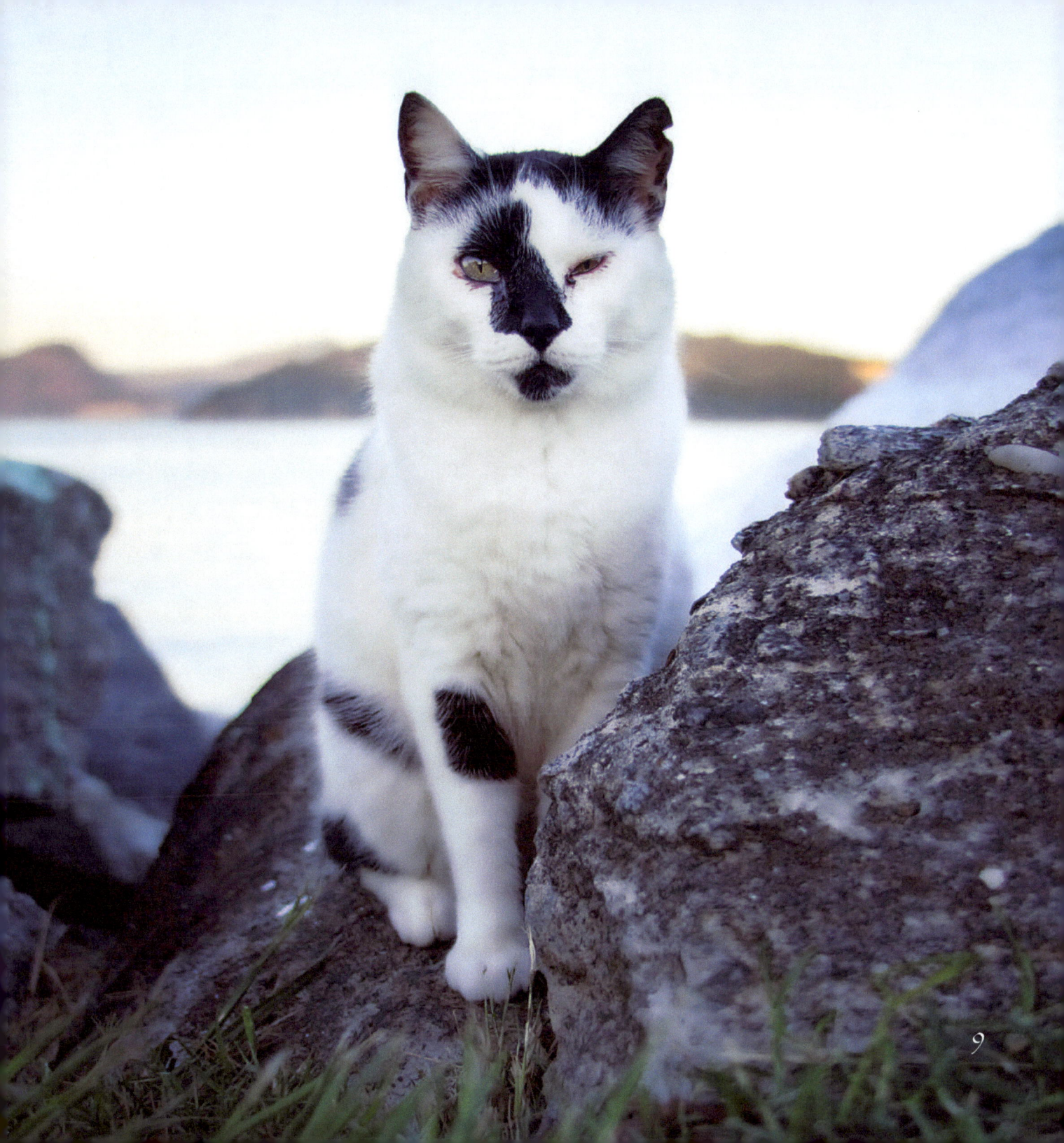

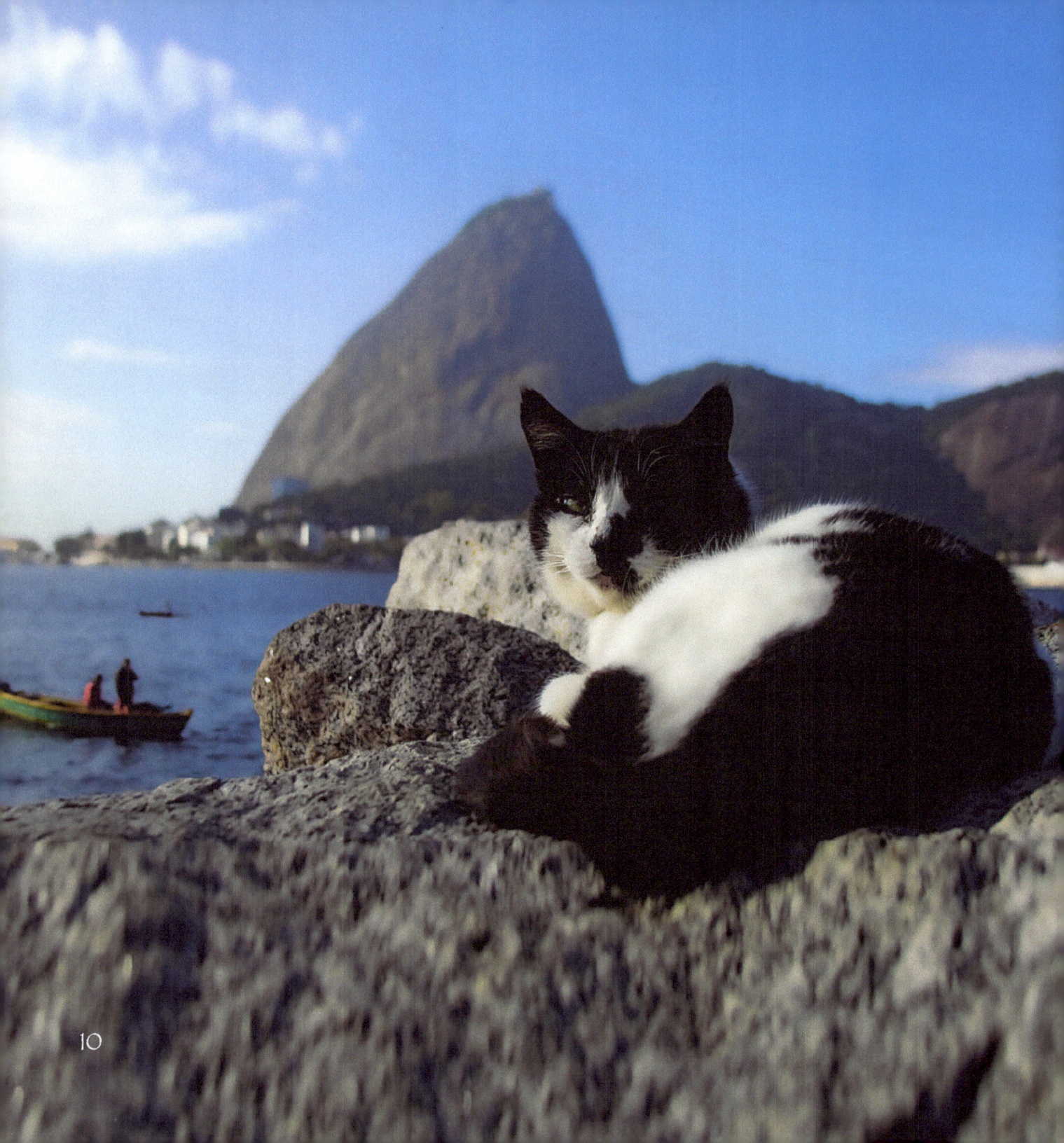

10

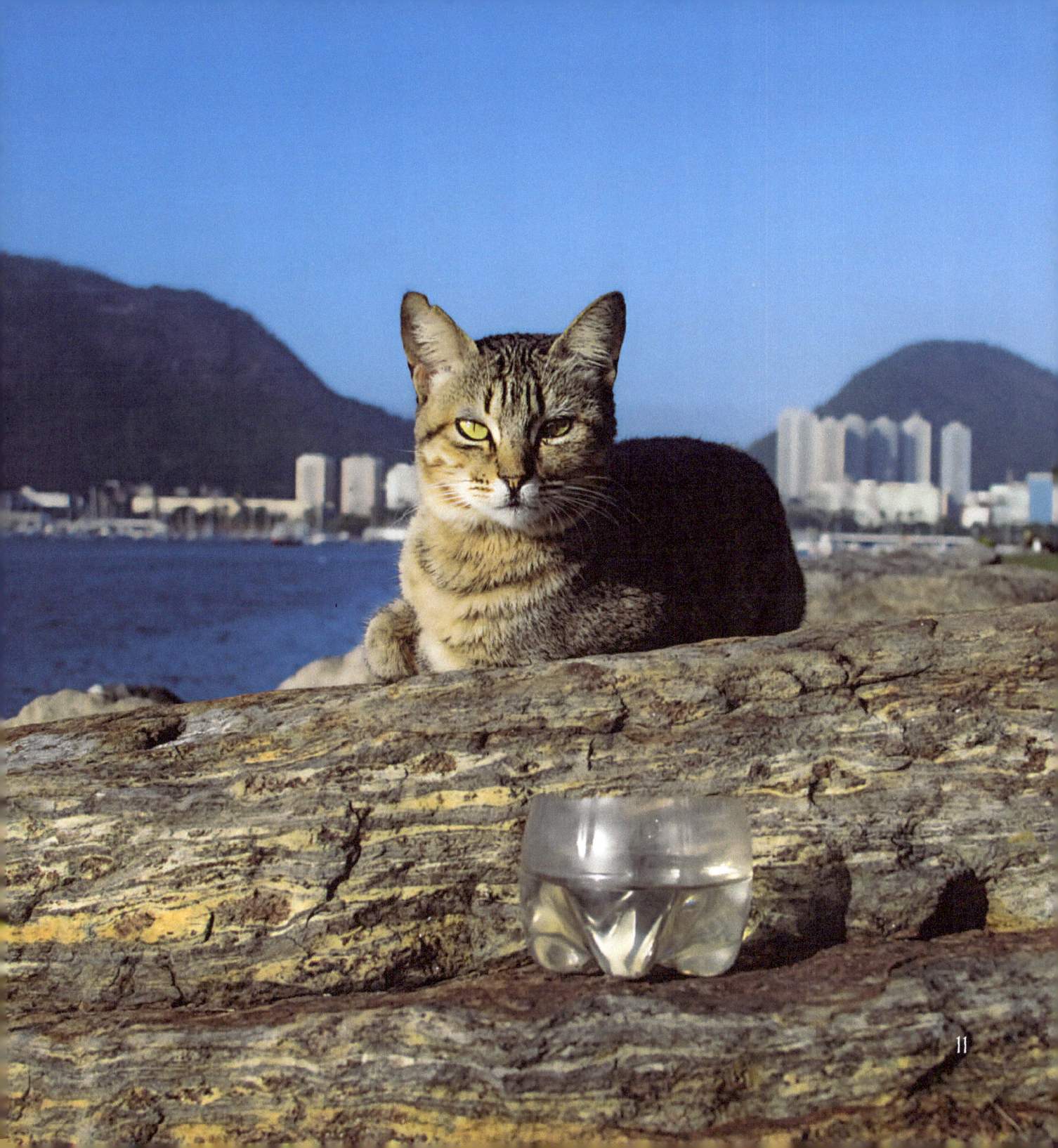

11

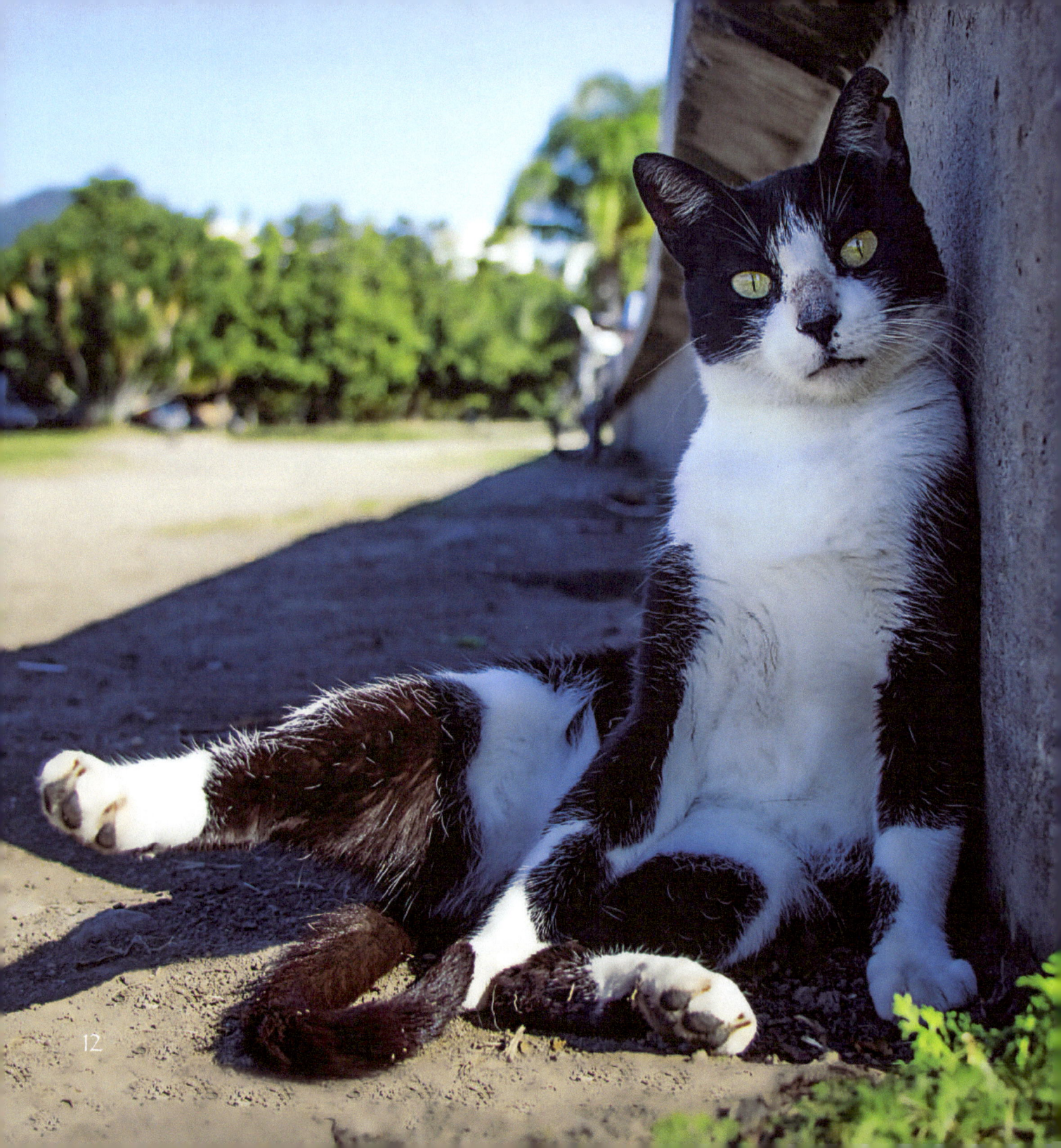

Brazil is the longest country in the world from north to south, spanning approximately 2,800 miles

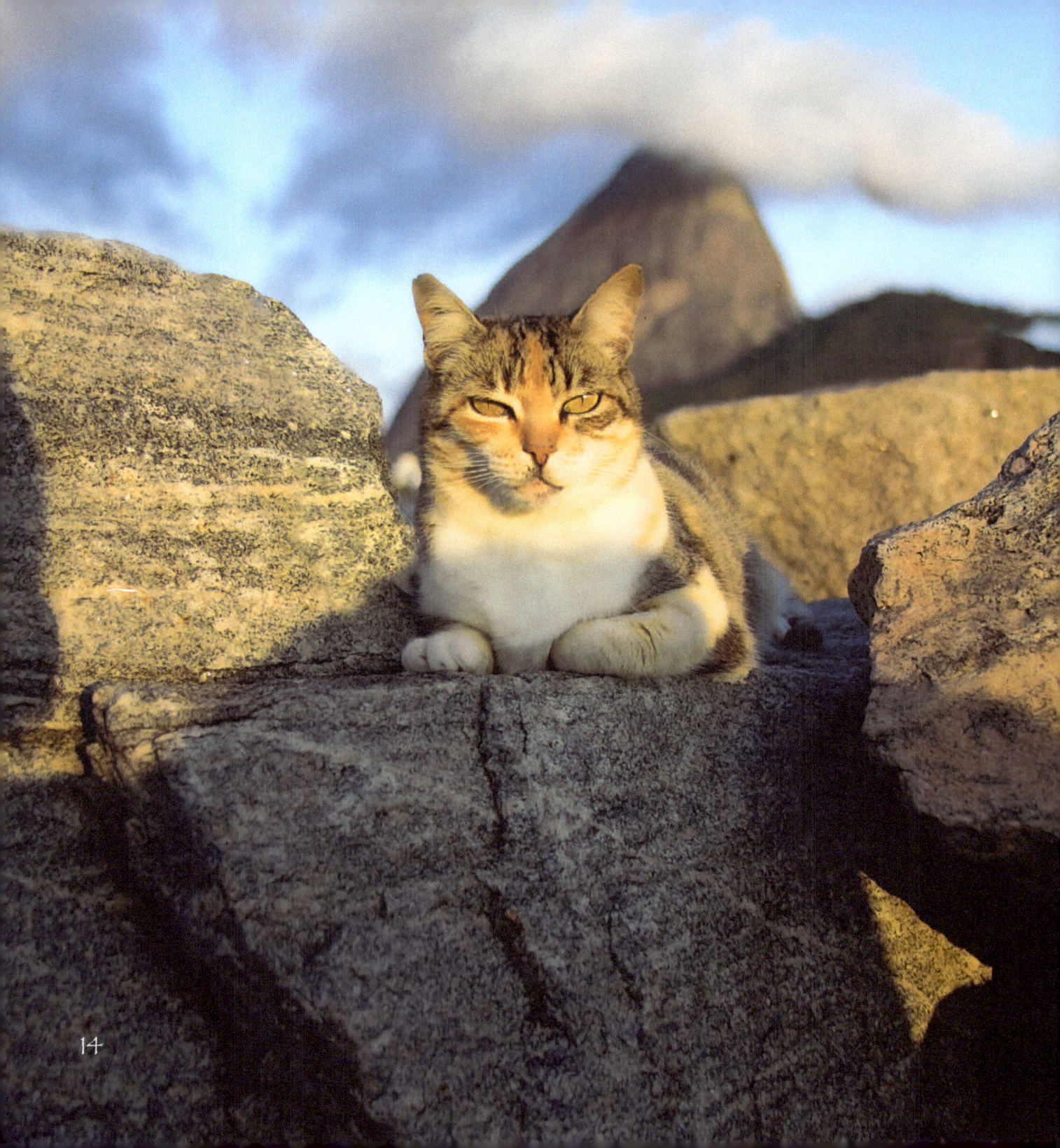

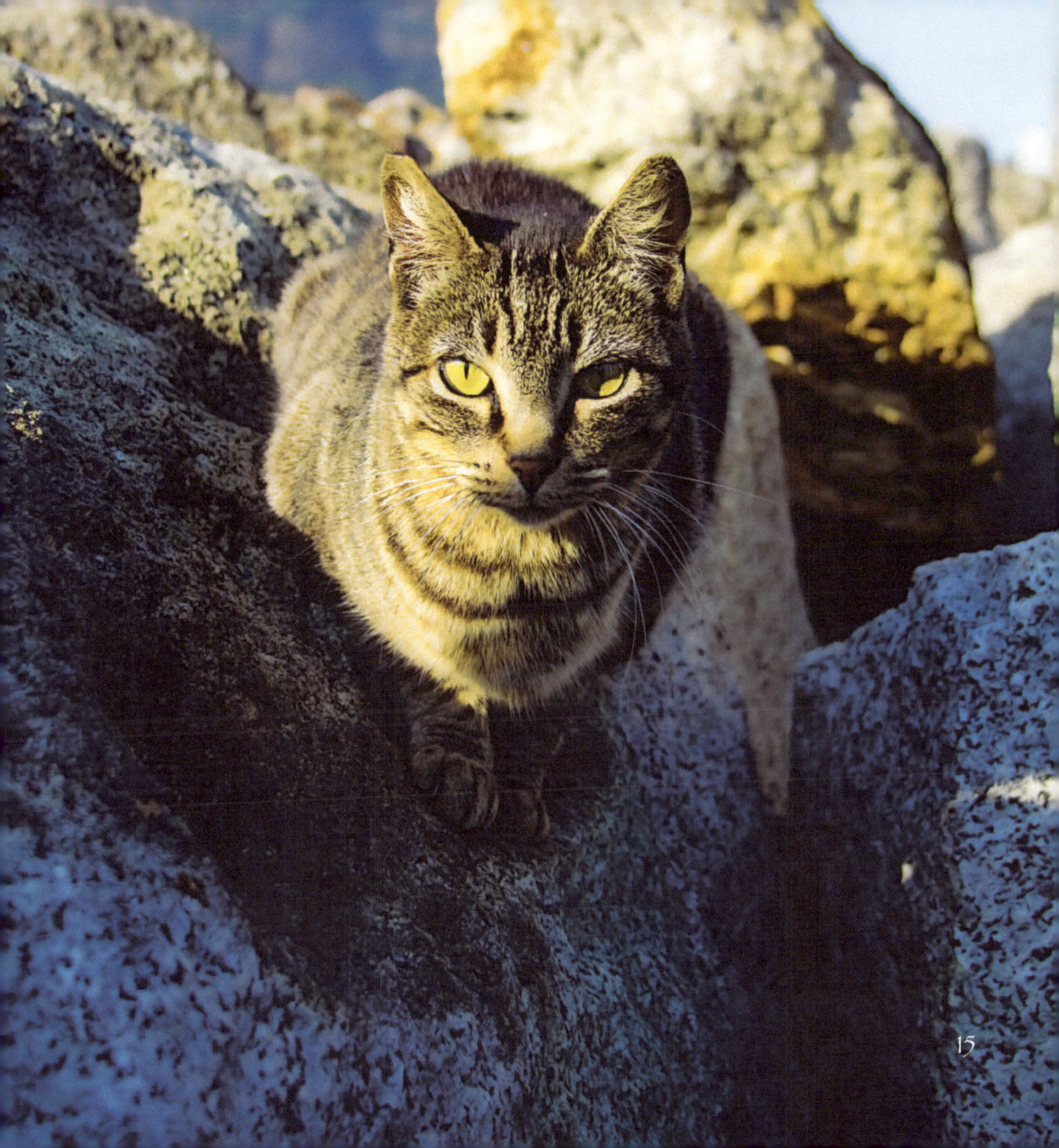

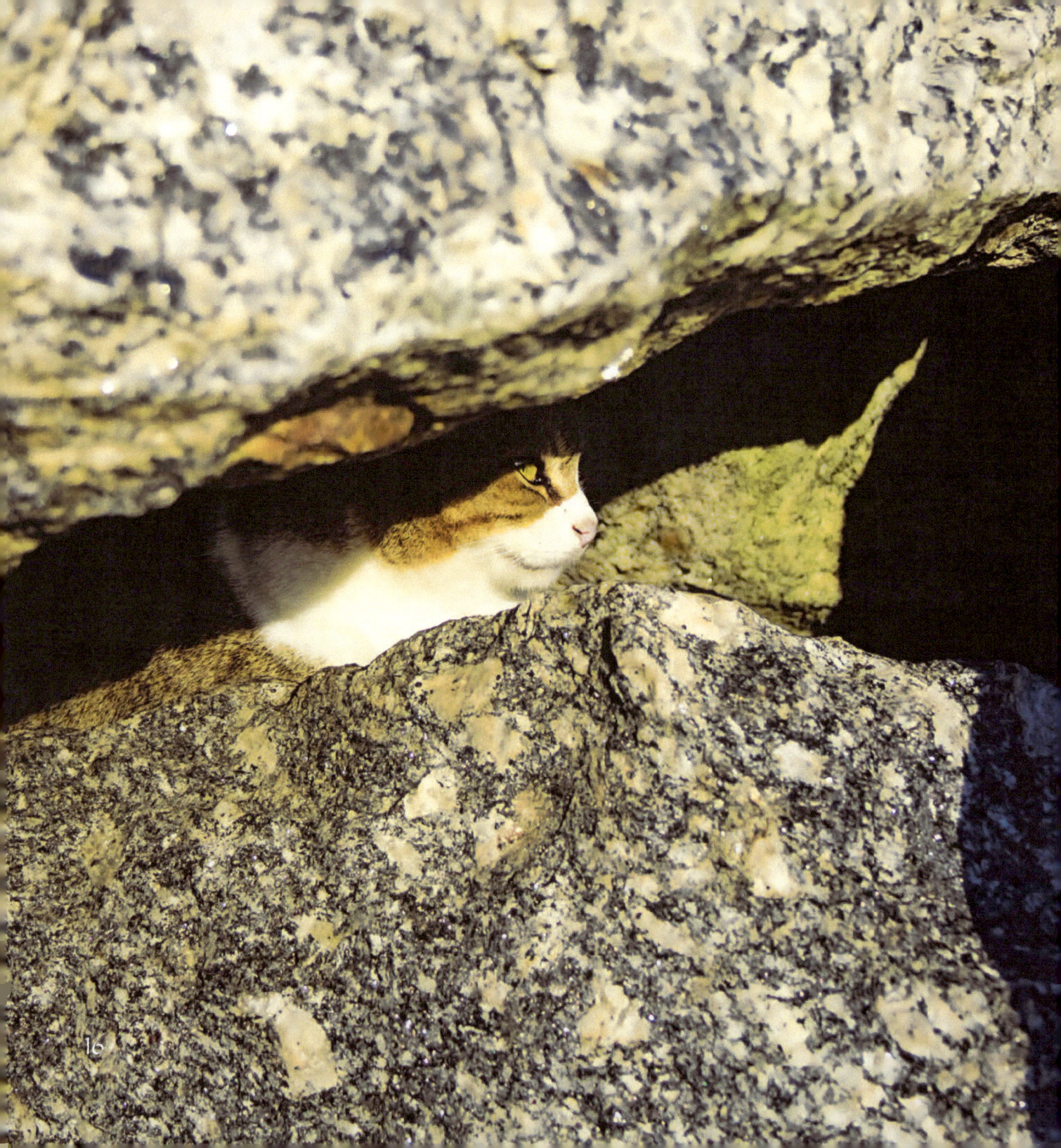

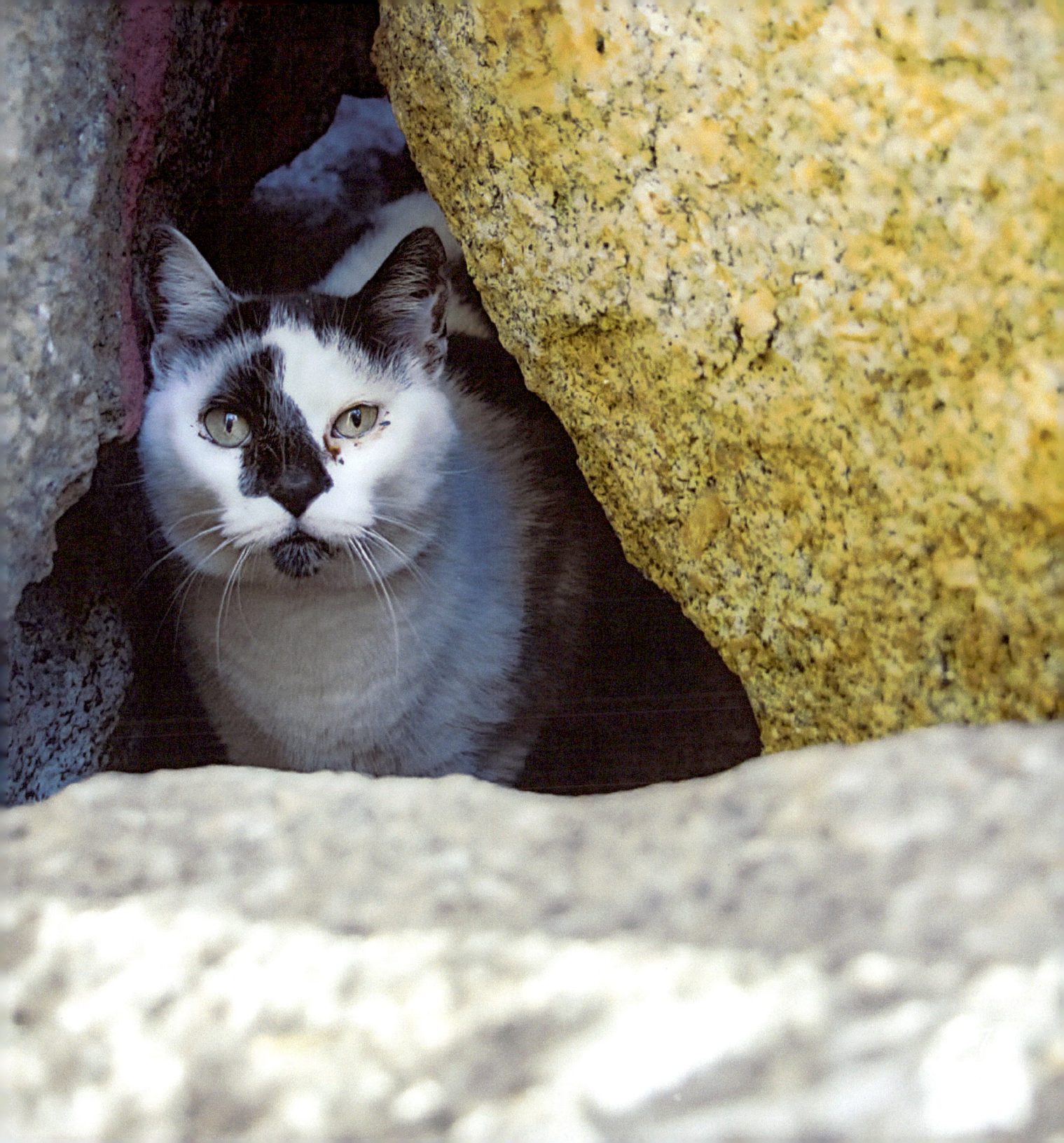

Cats born with 6 or 7 front toes and extra back toe are called polydactl

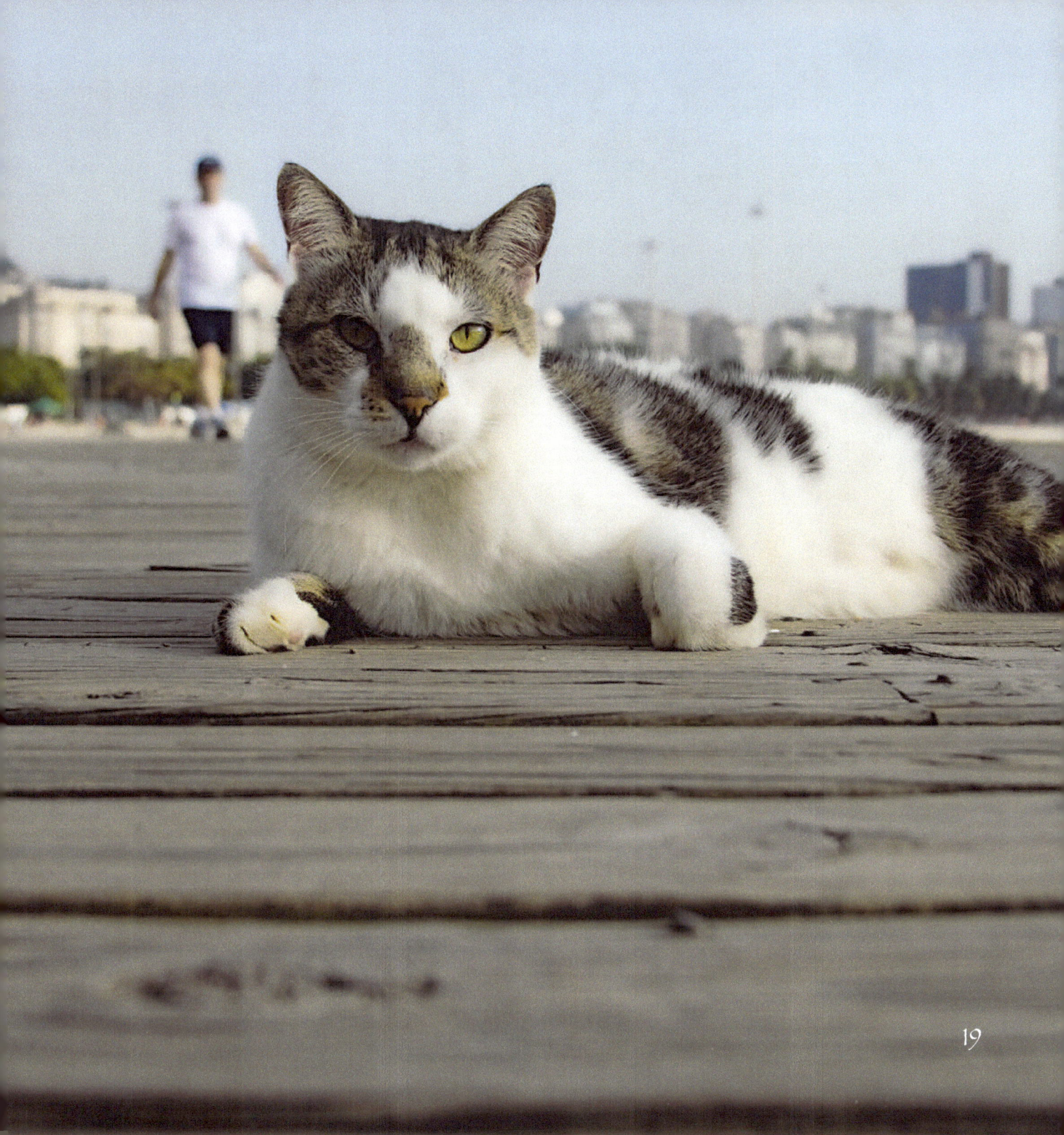

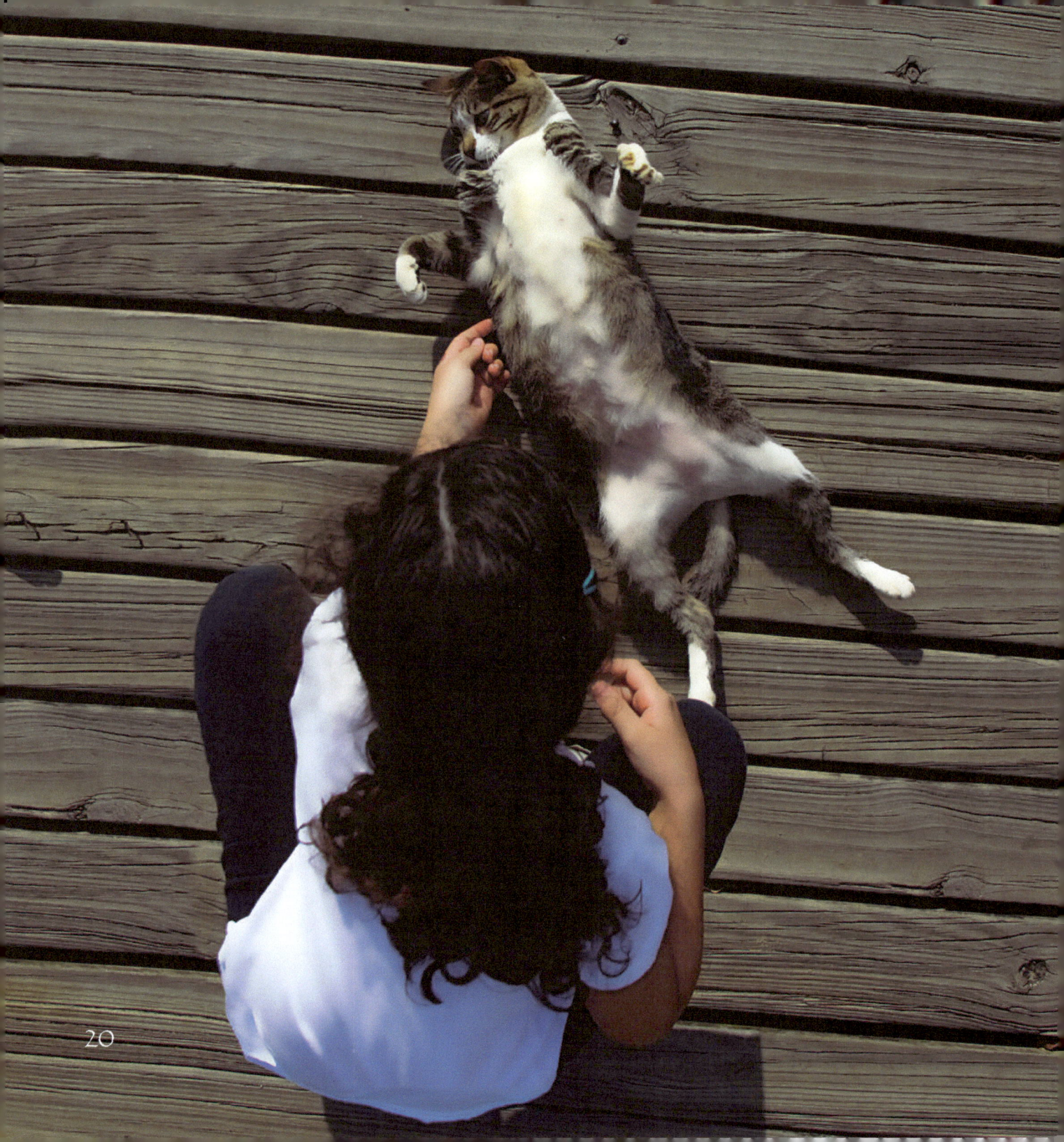

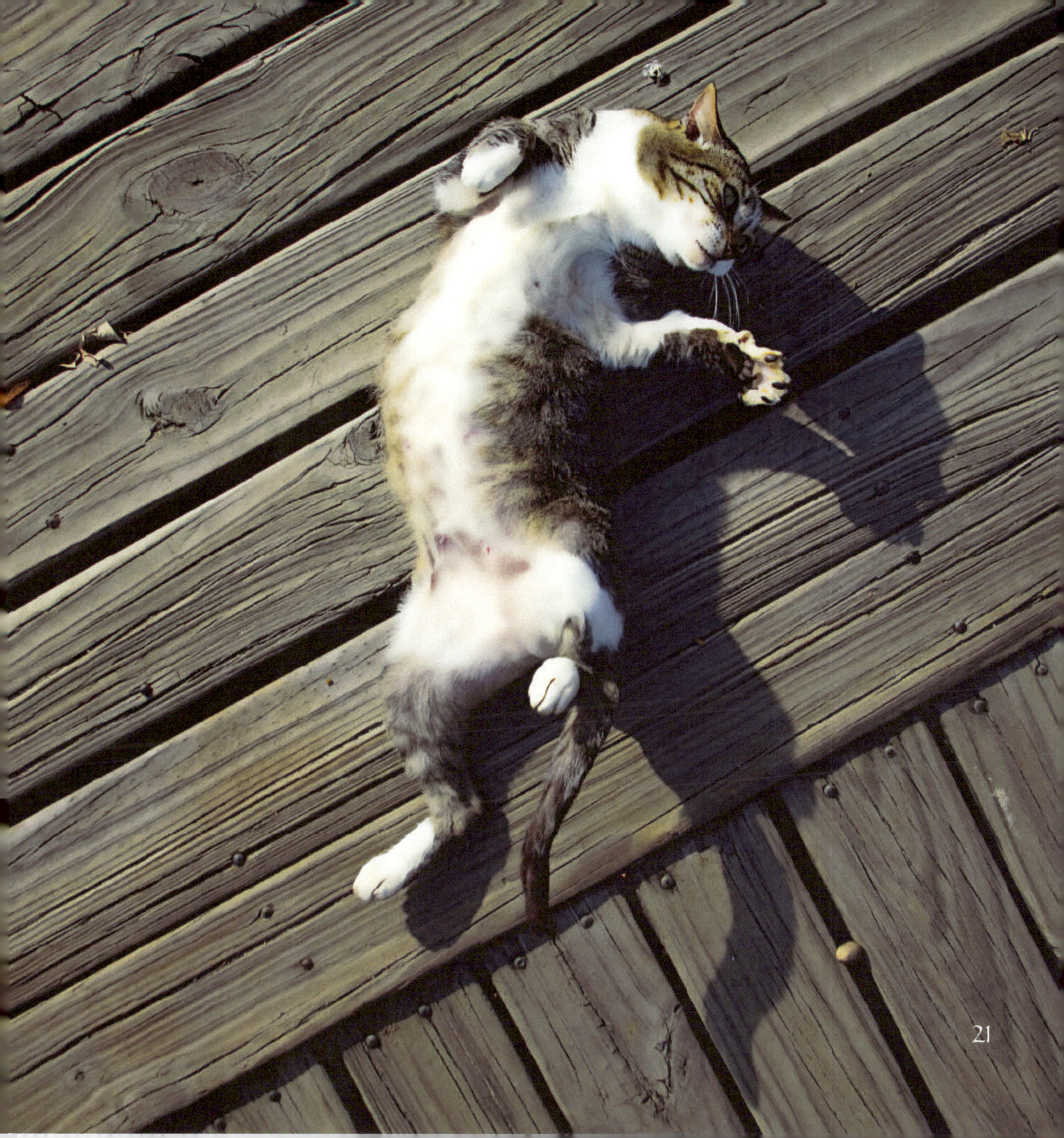

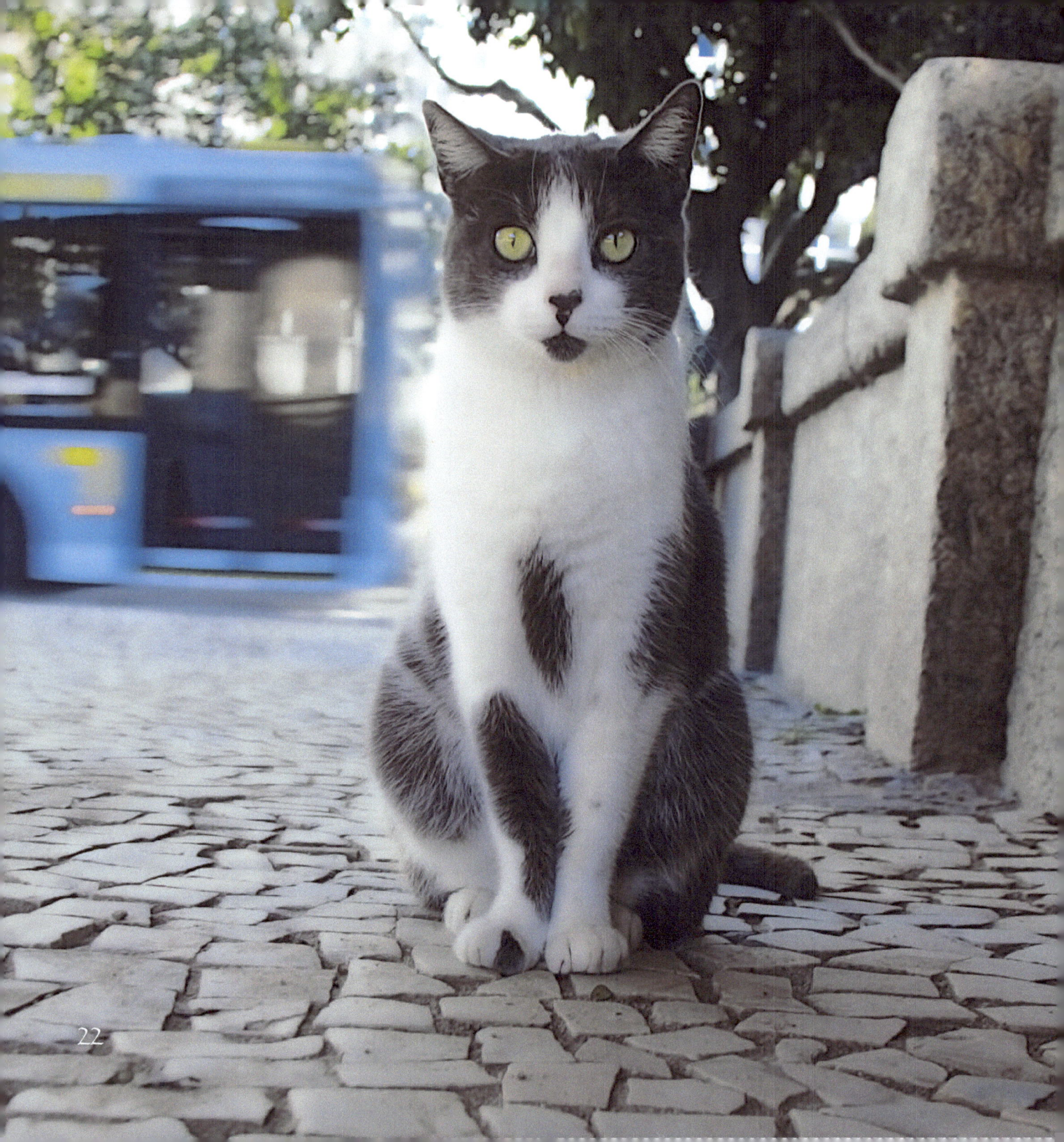

Brazil's National Library is located in Rio de Janeiro at Cinelandia square and is the largest library in South America

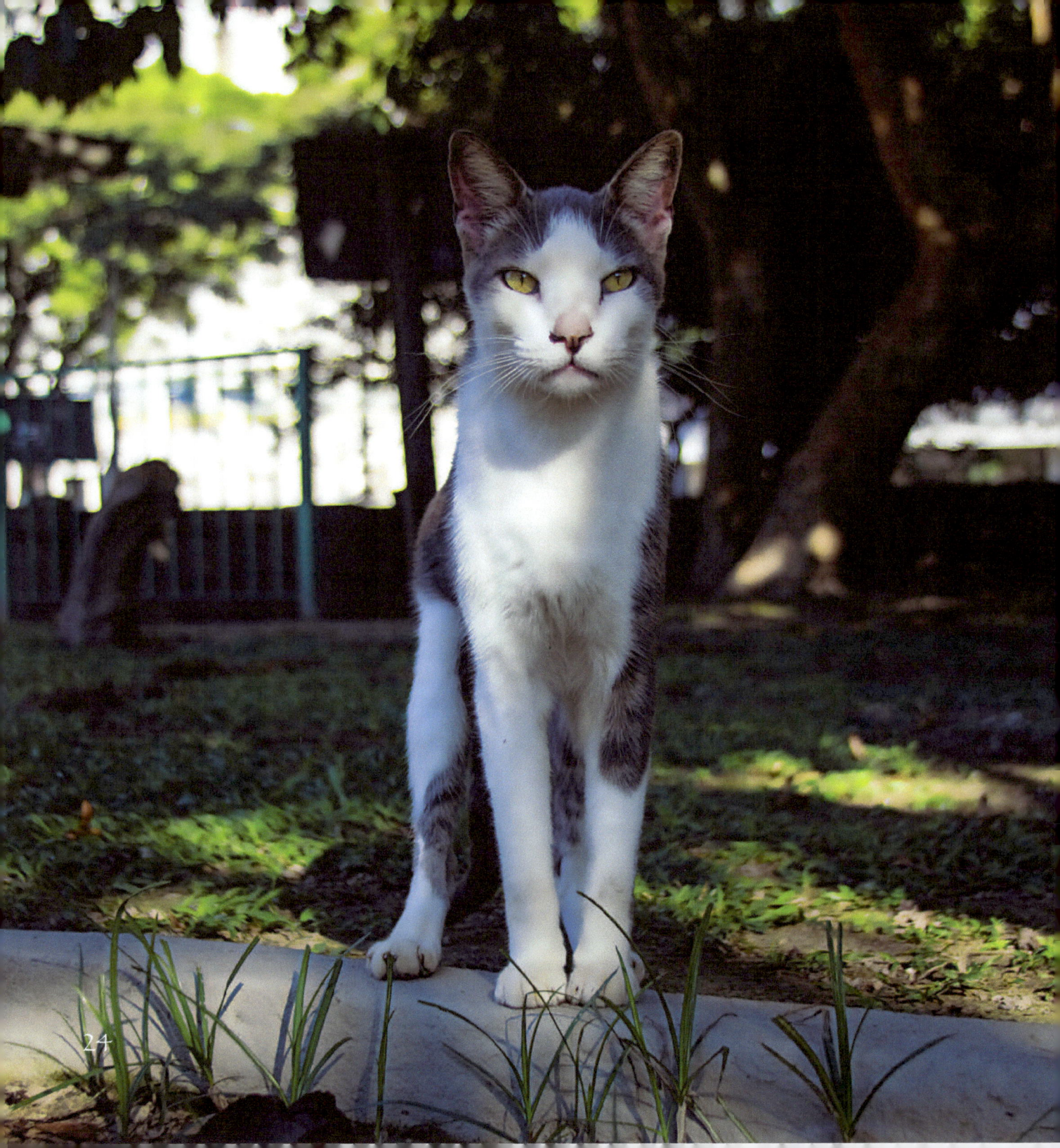

24

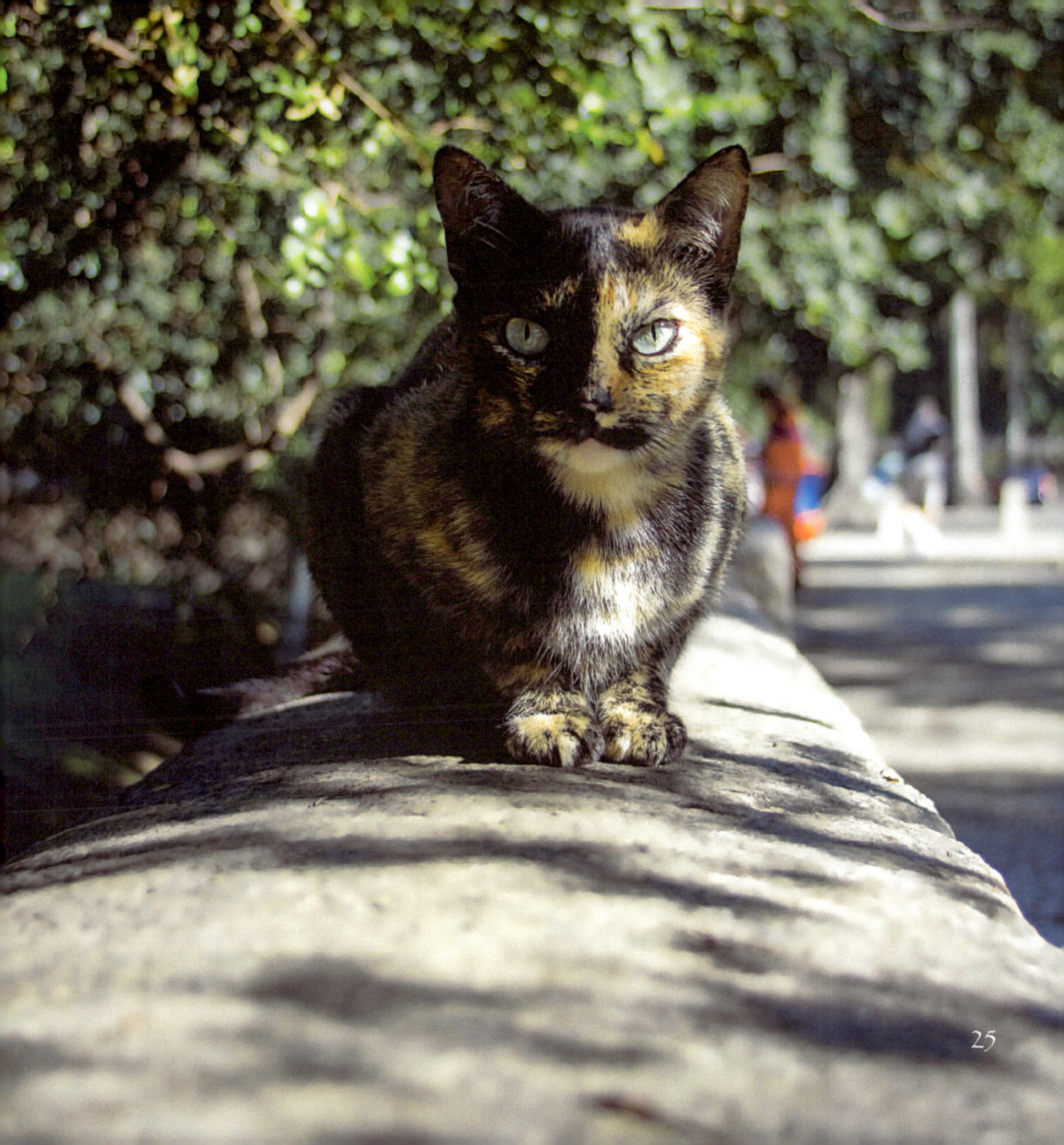

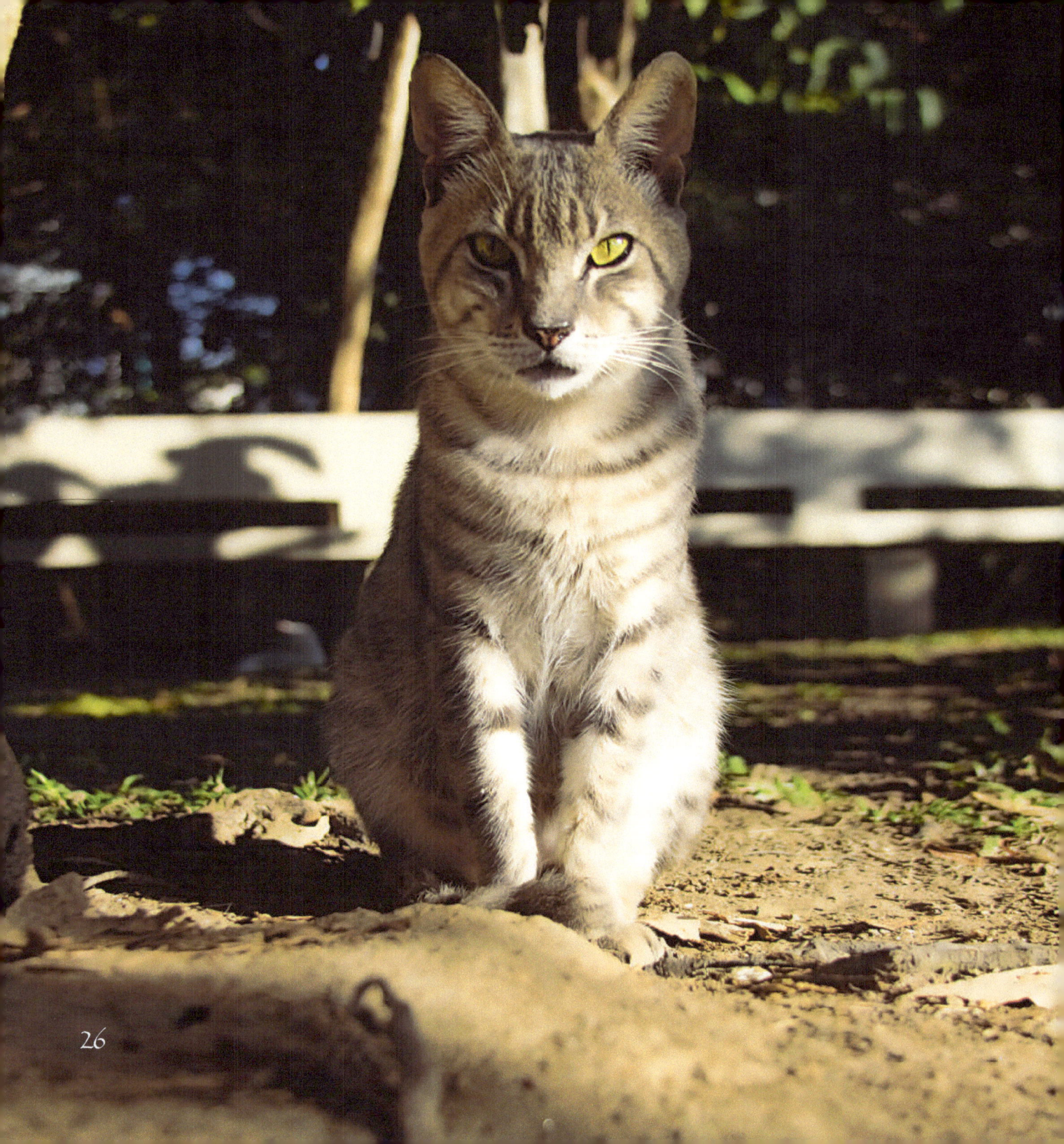

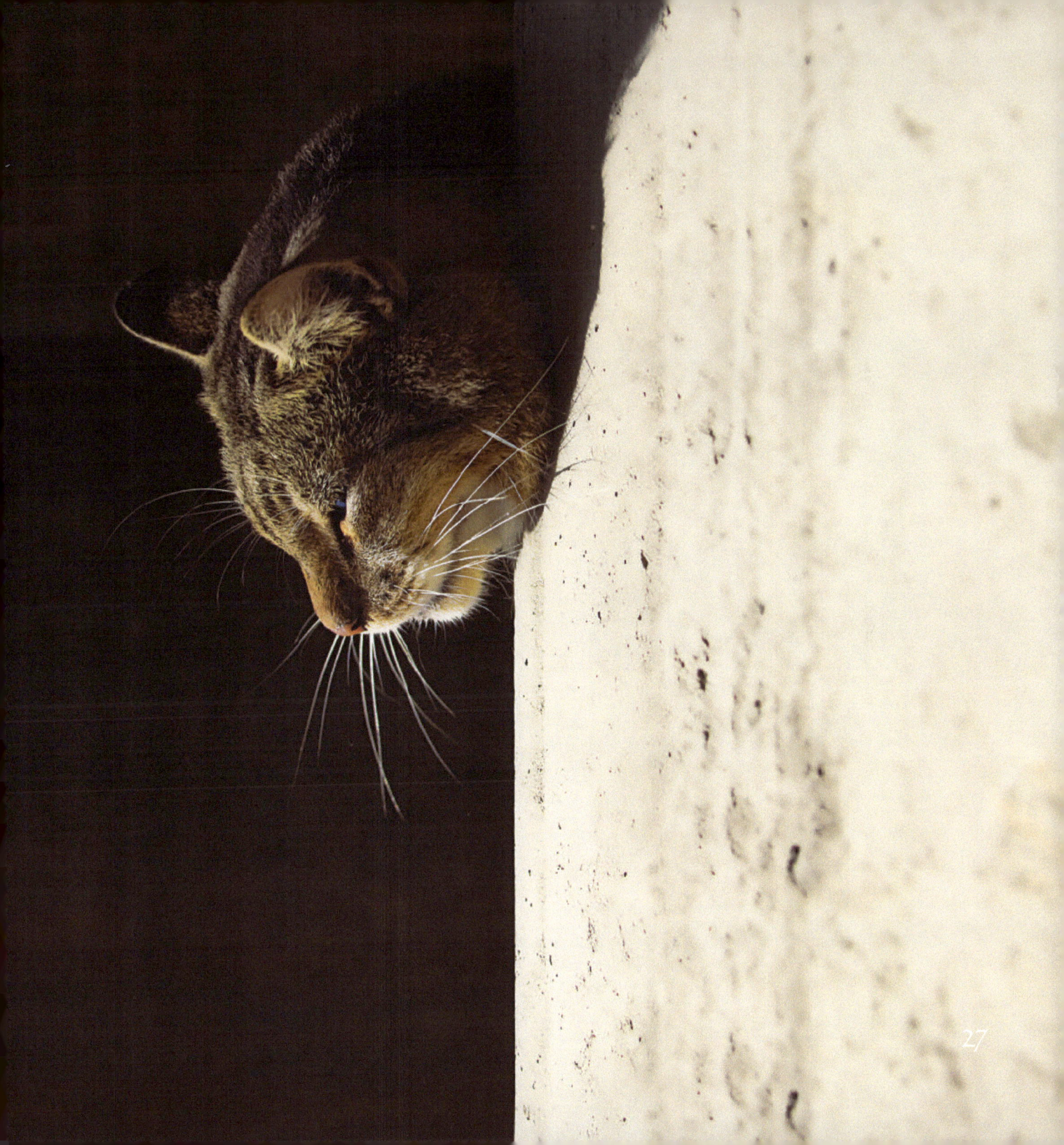

The world's rarest coffee, Kopi Luwak, comes from an Indonesia wildcat called the Luwak that eats coffee berries and the beans are then harvested from the cat's dung, cleaned and roasted

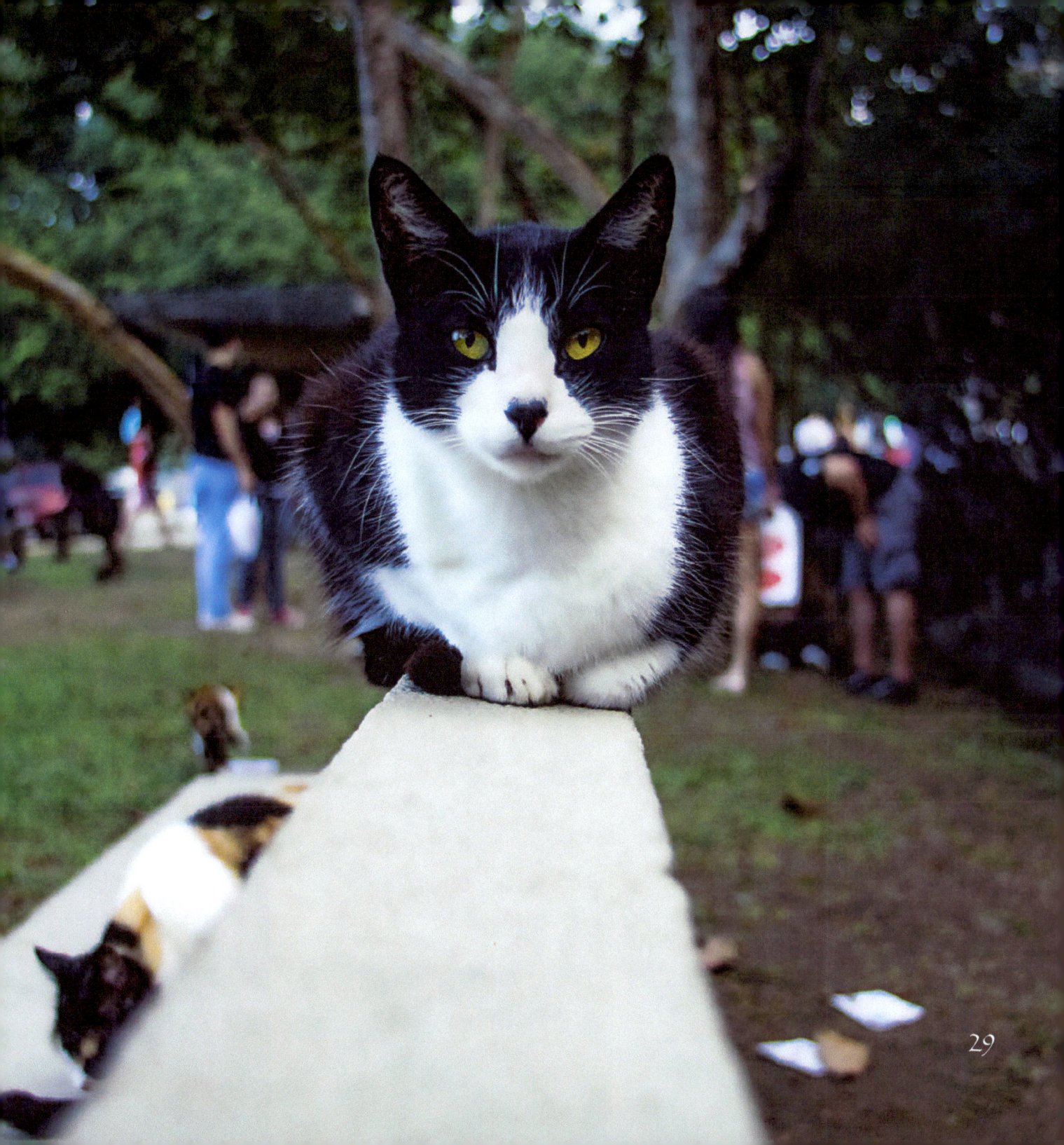

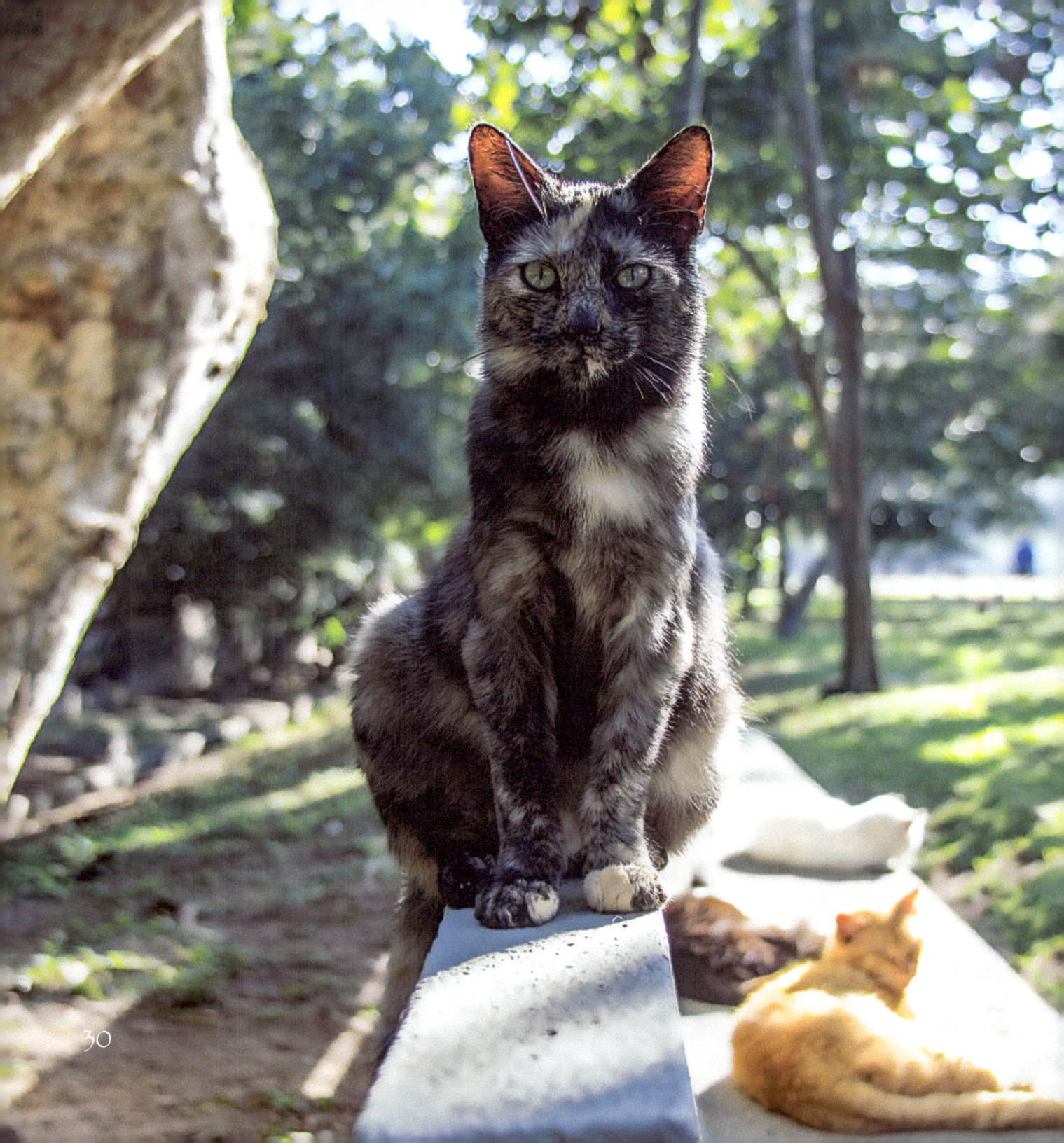

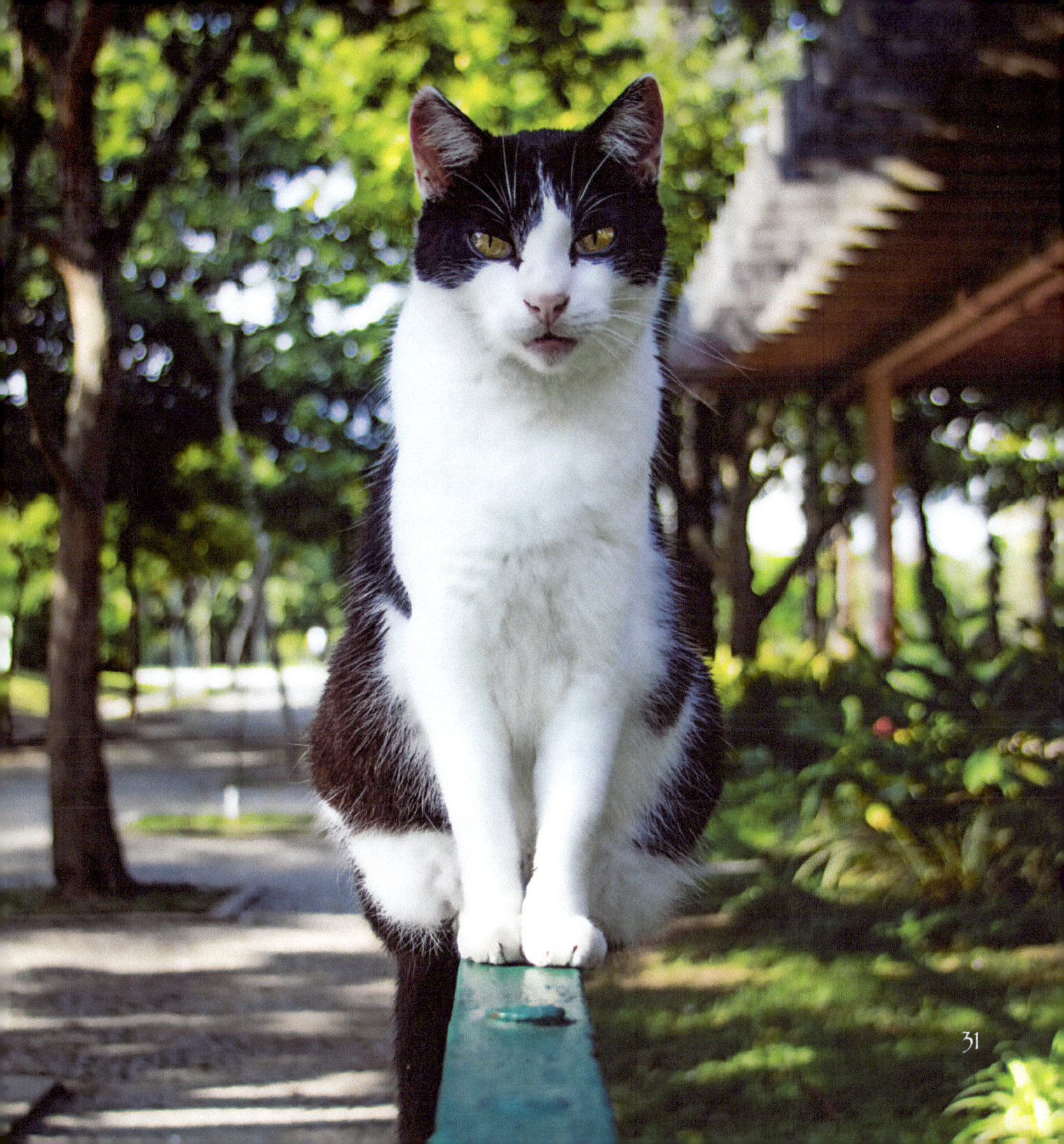

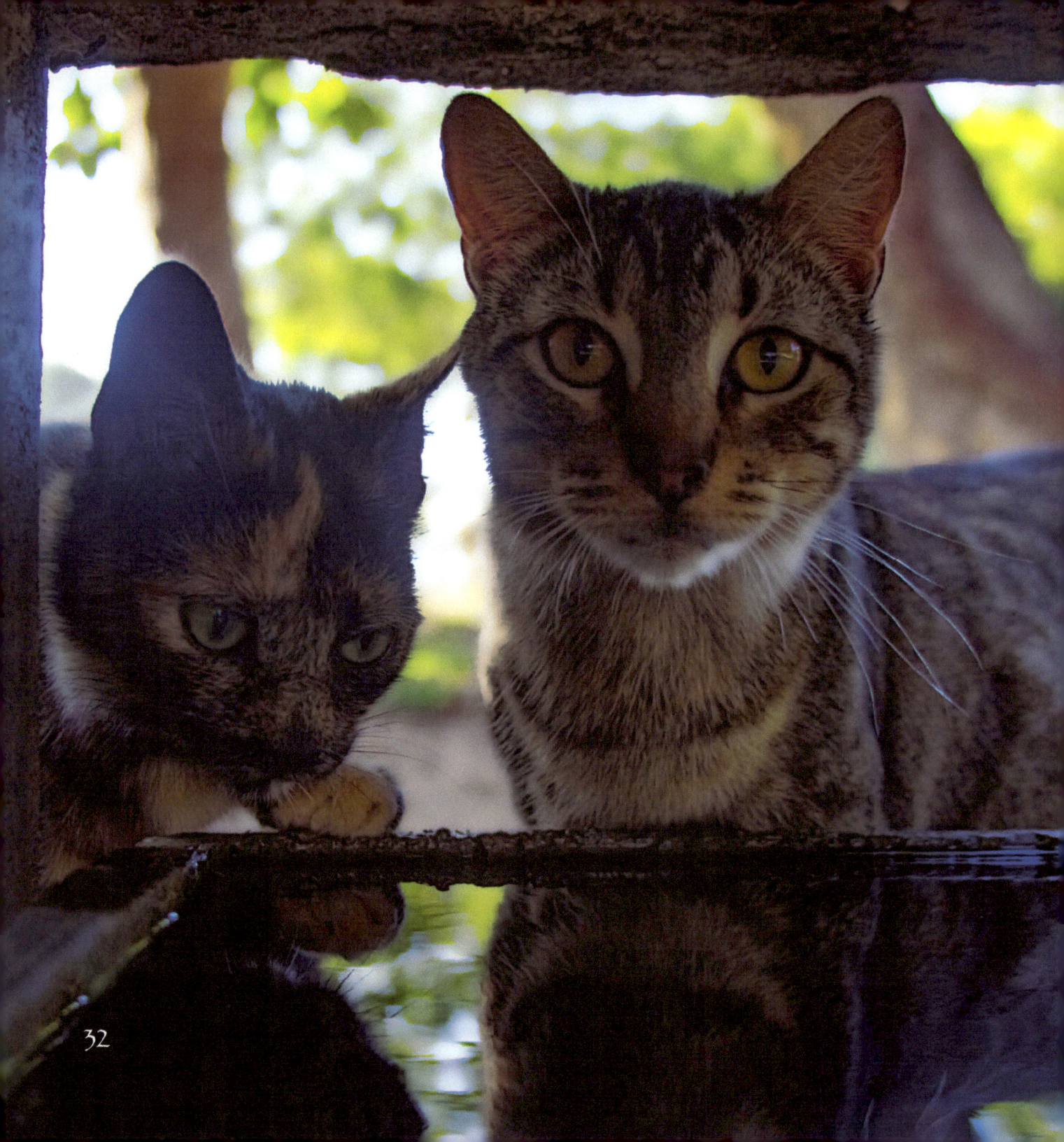

Rio's locals are called Carioca, meaning white man's house, the word was given to the Portuguese colonist by the indigenous Indians

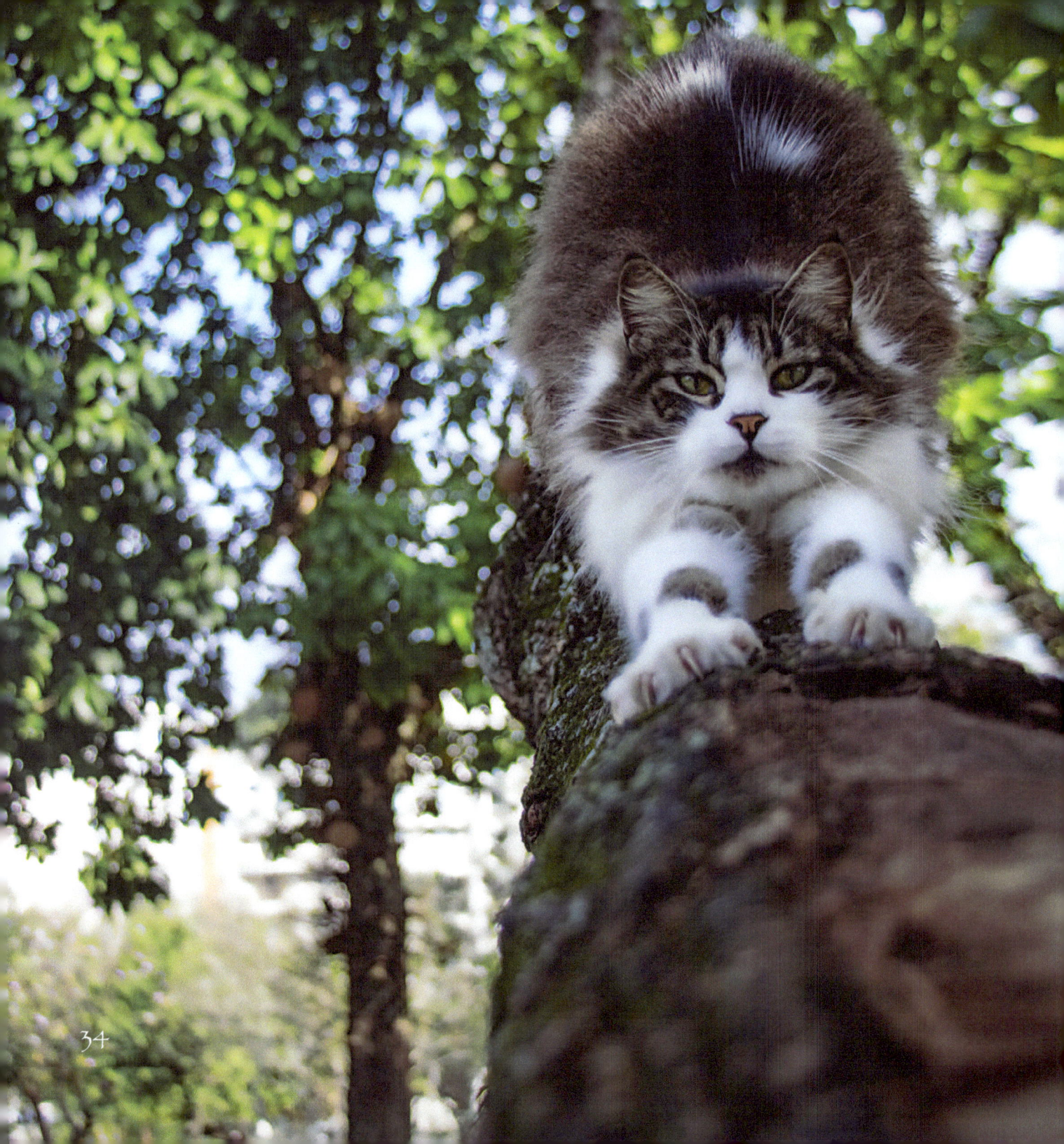

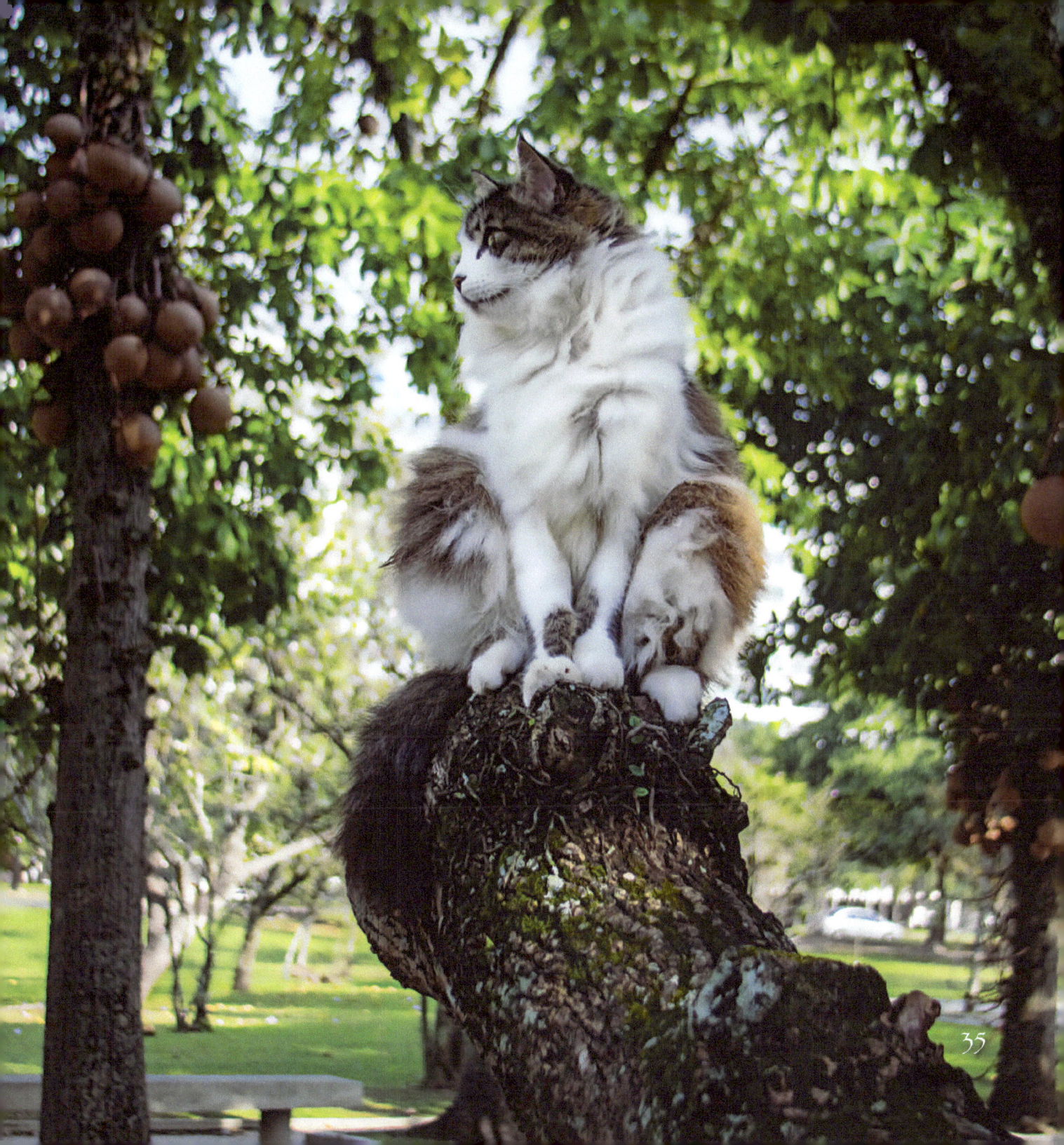

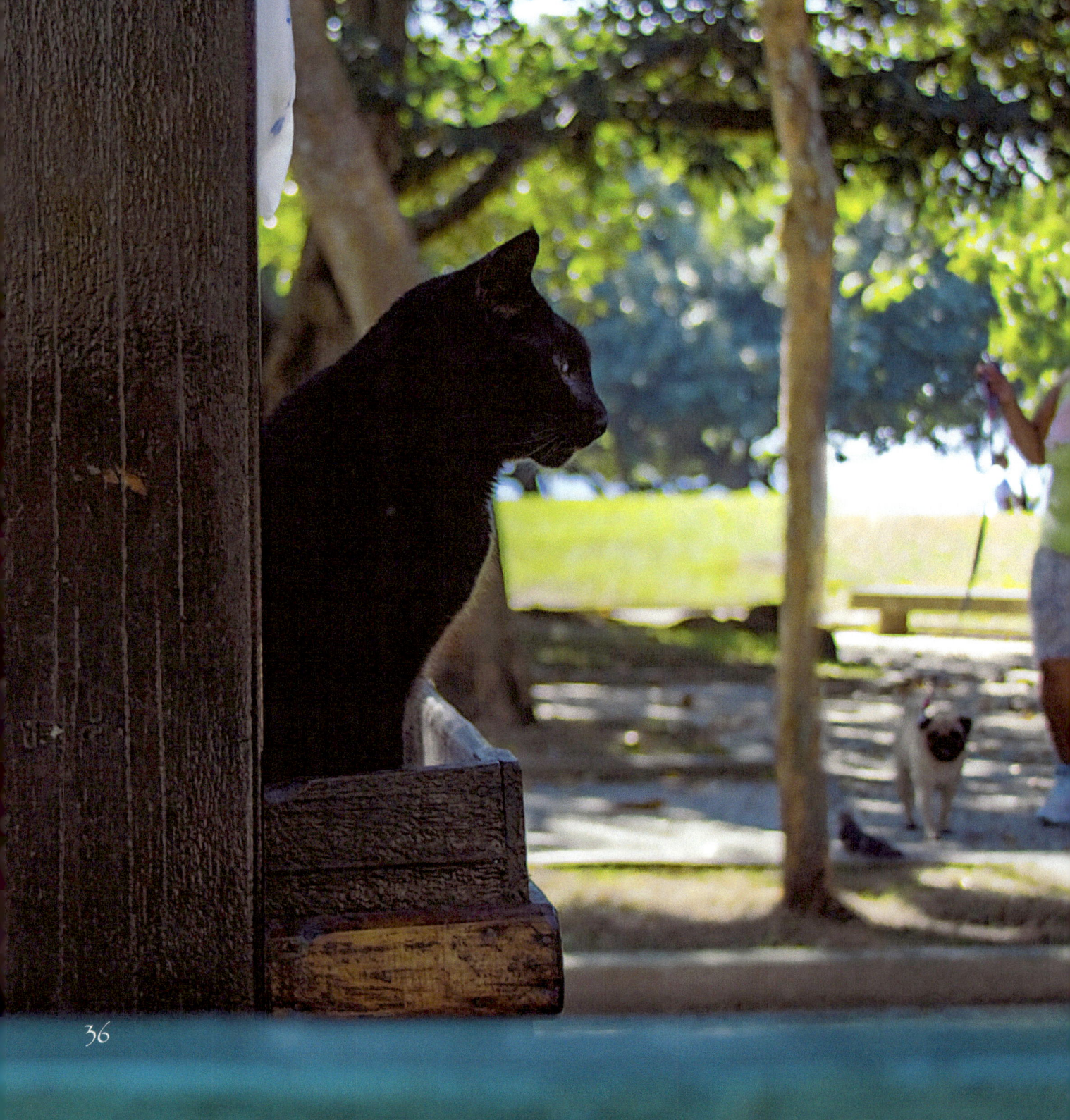

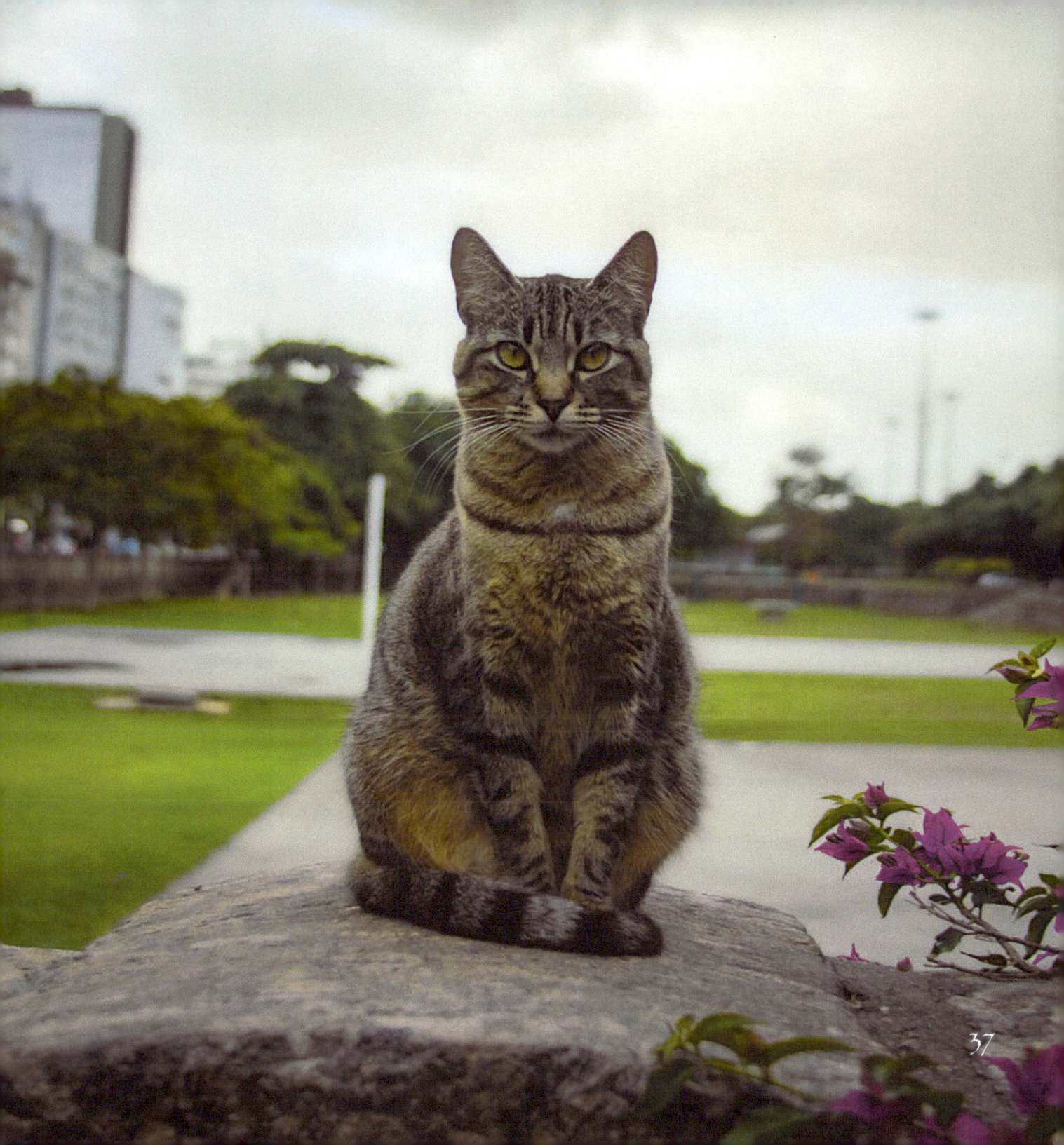

On average a cat will sleep for 16 hours a day

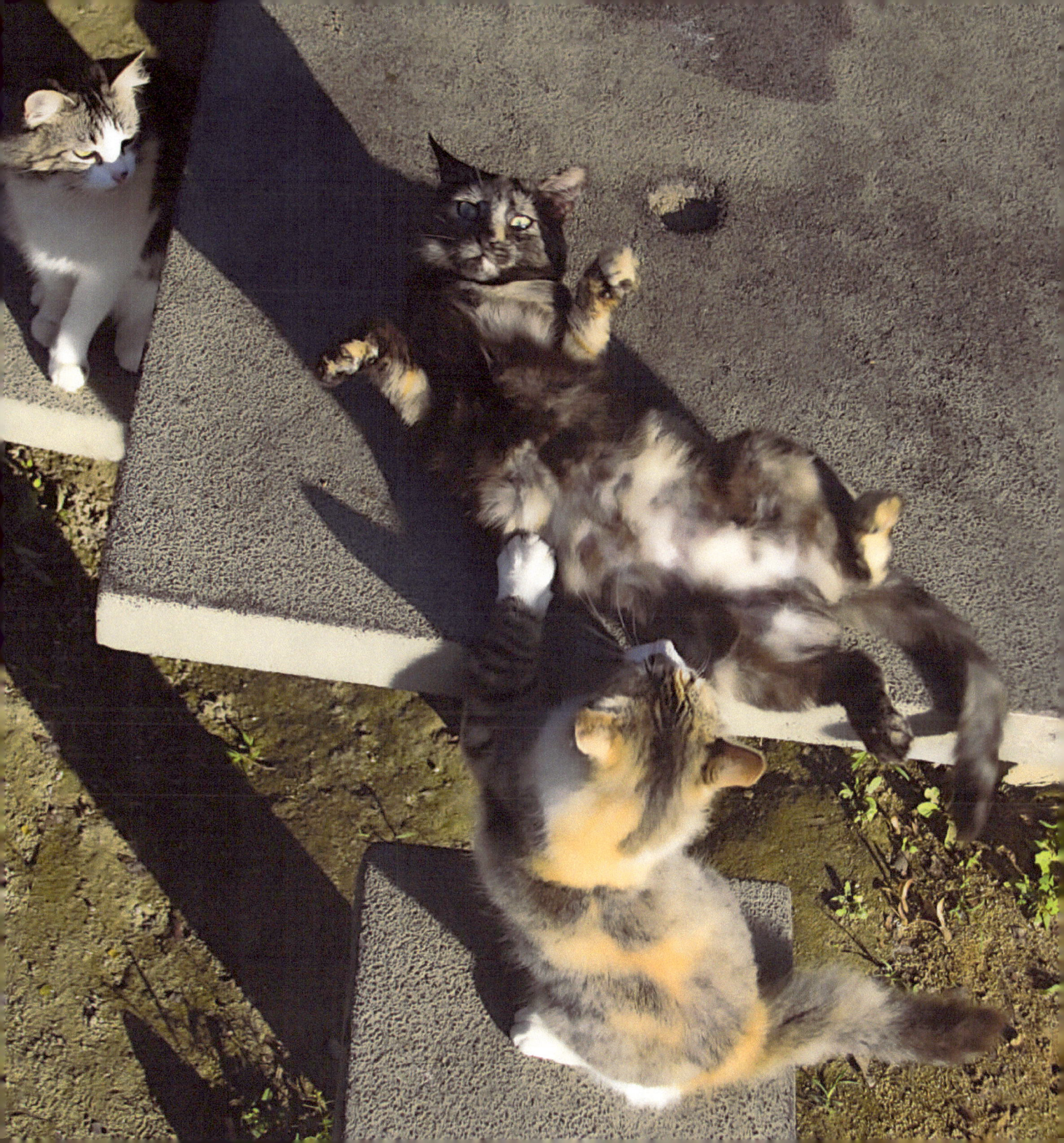

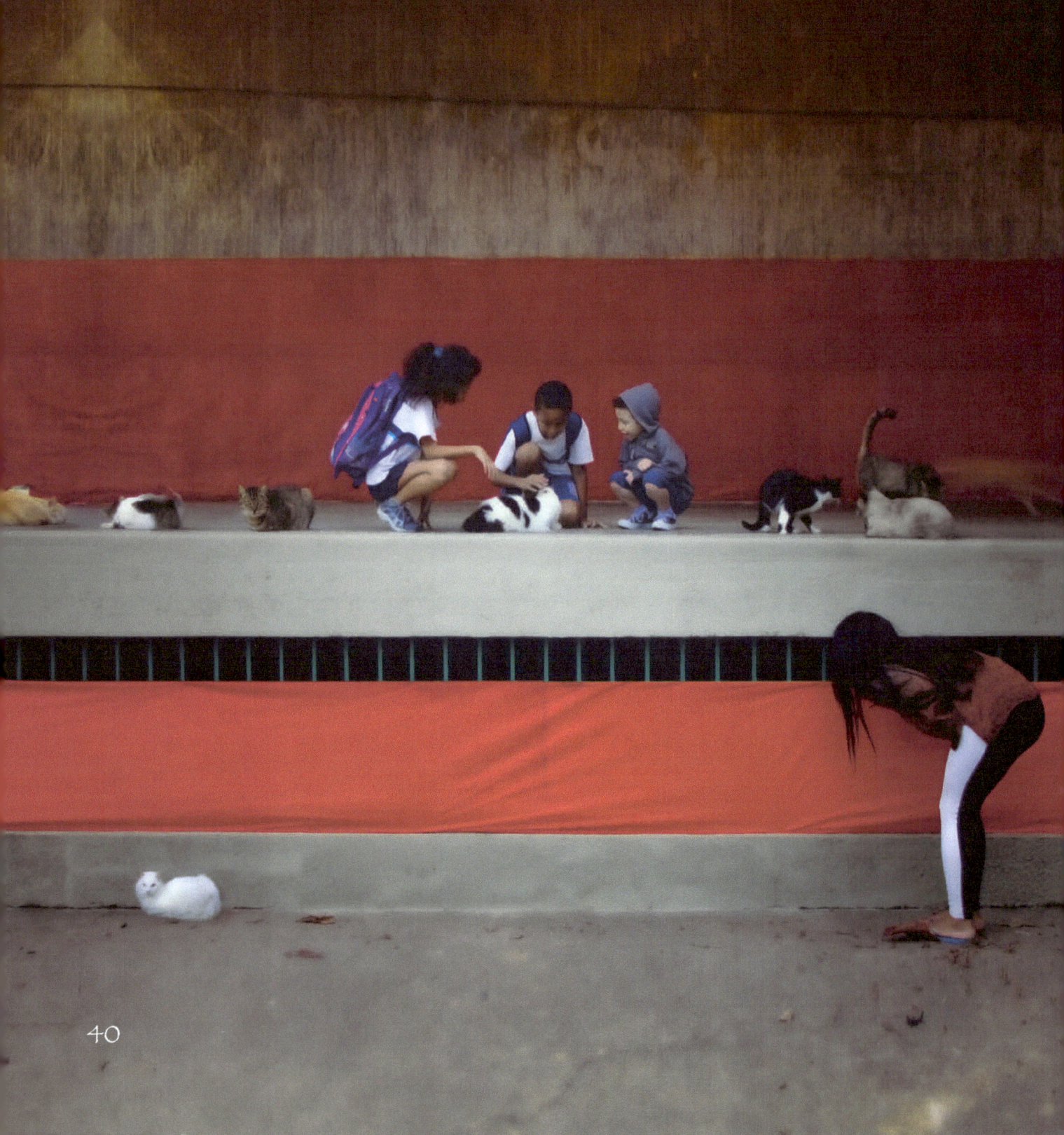

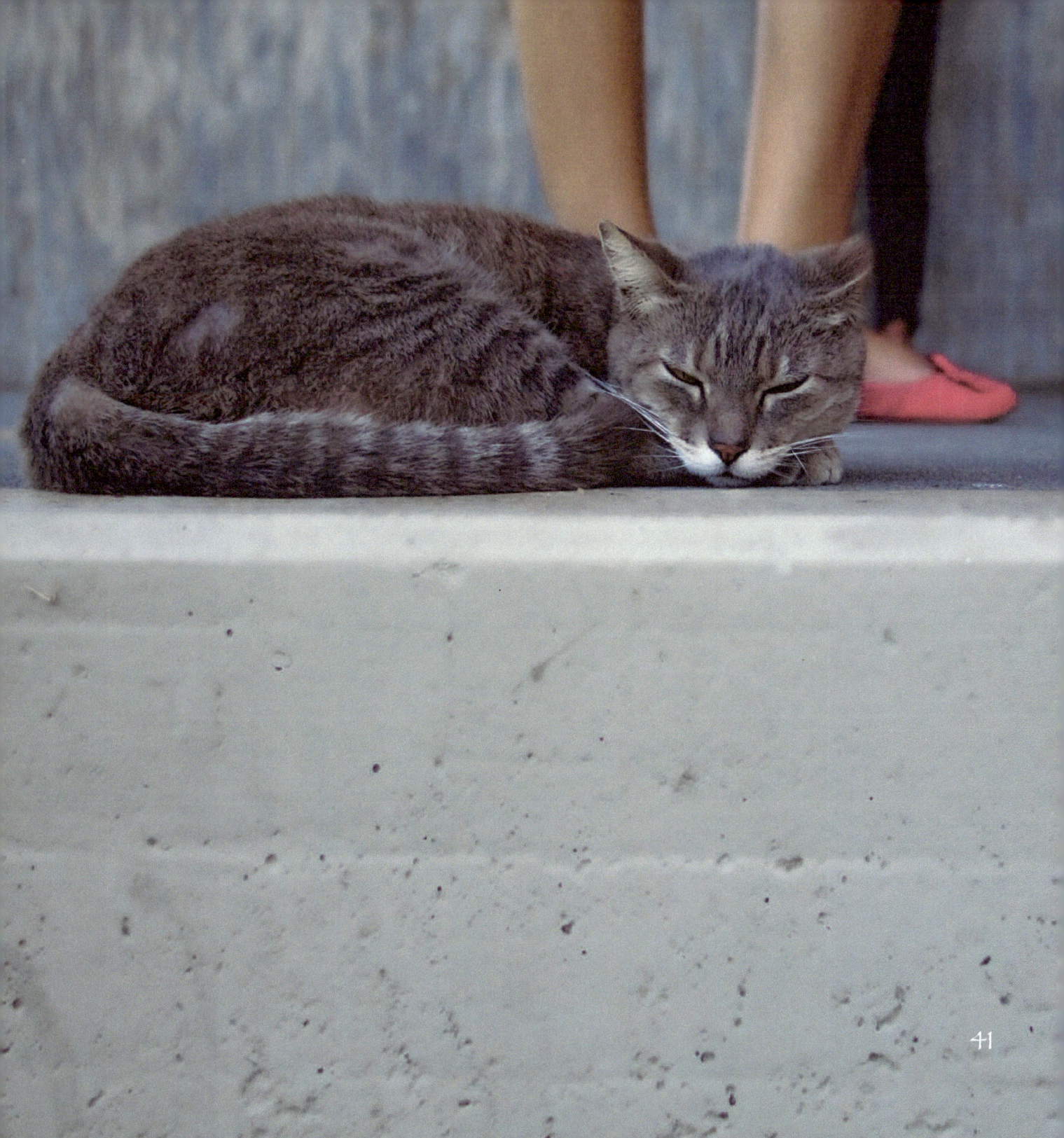

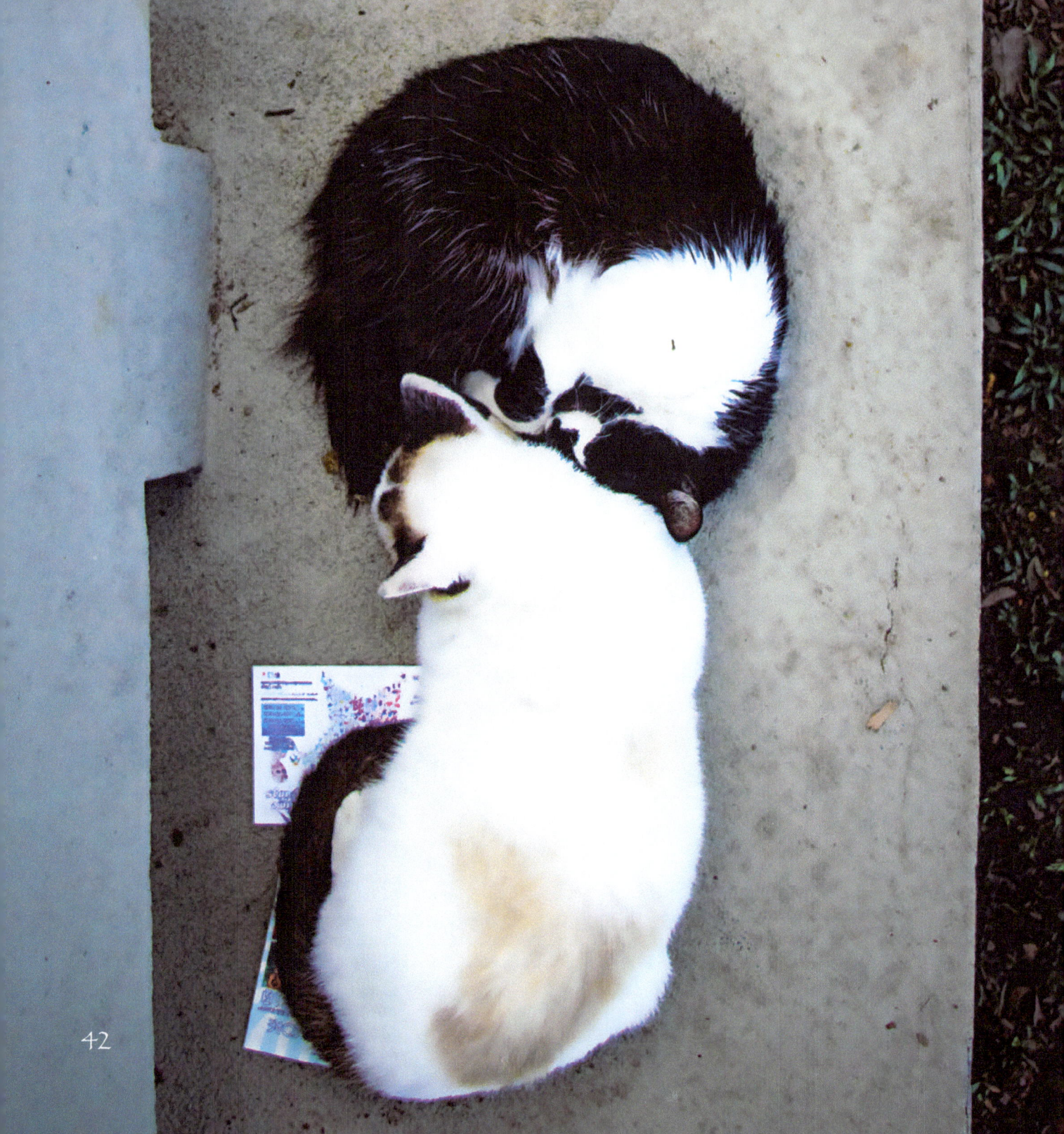

Brazil contains almost 60 percent of the Amazon rain forest

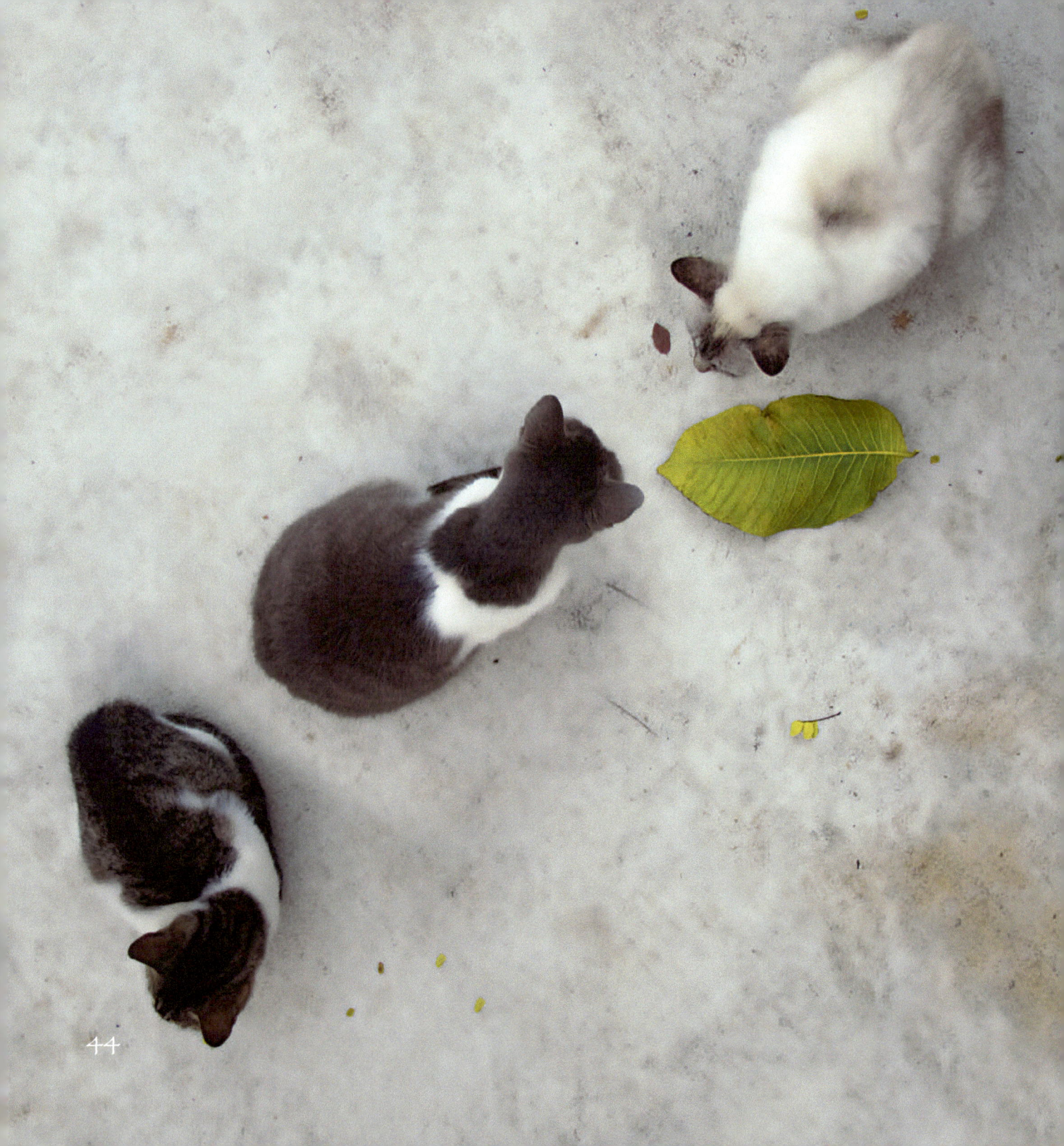

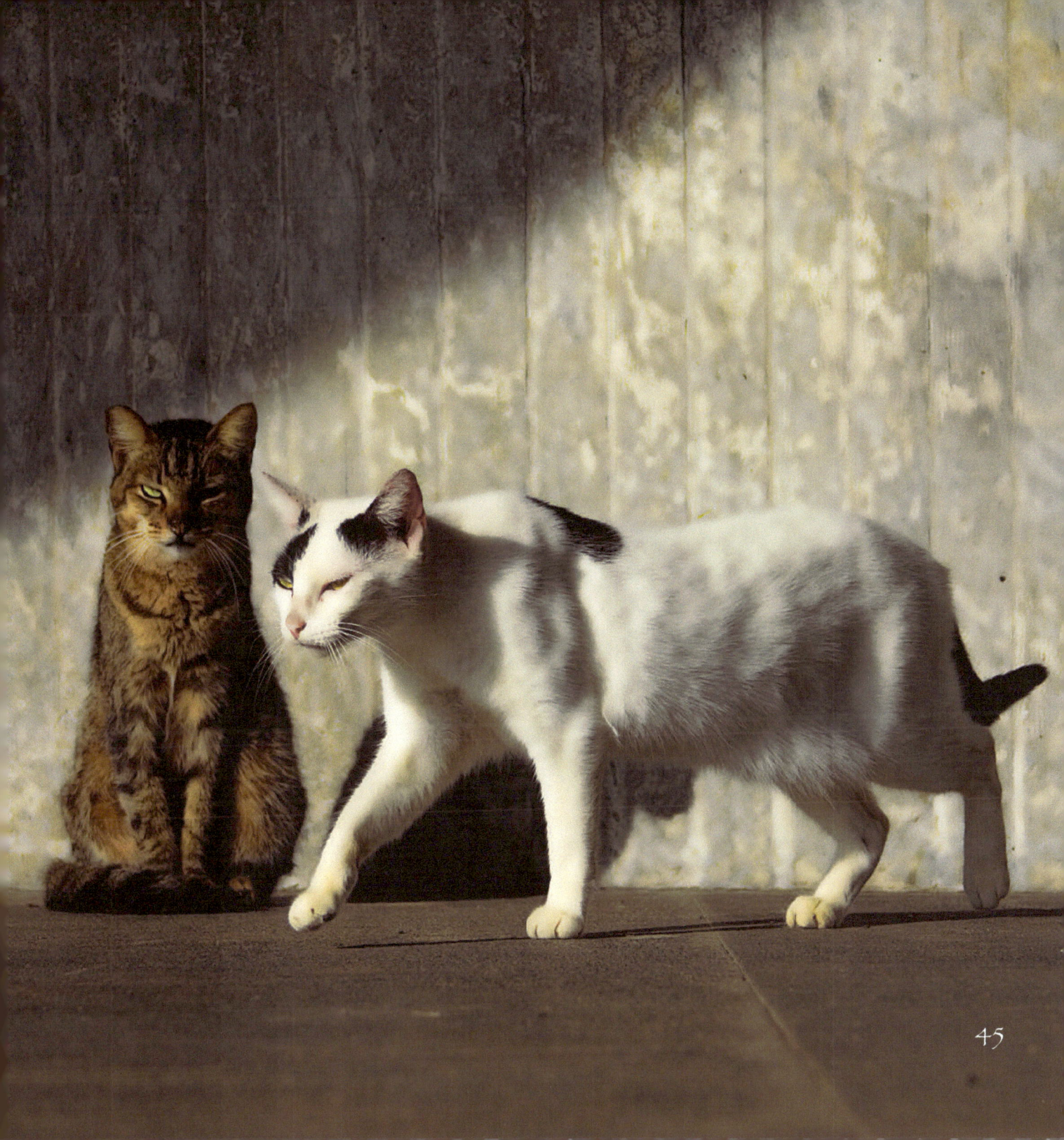

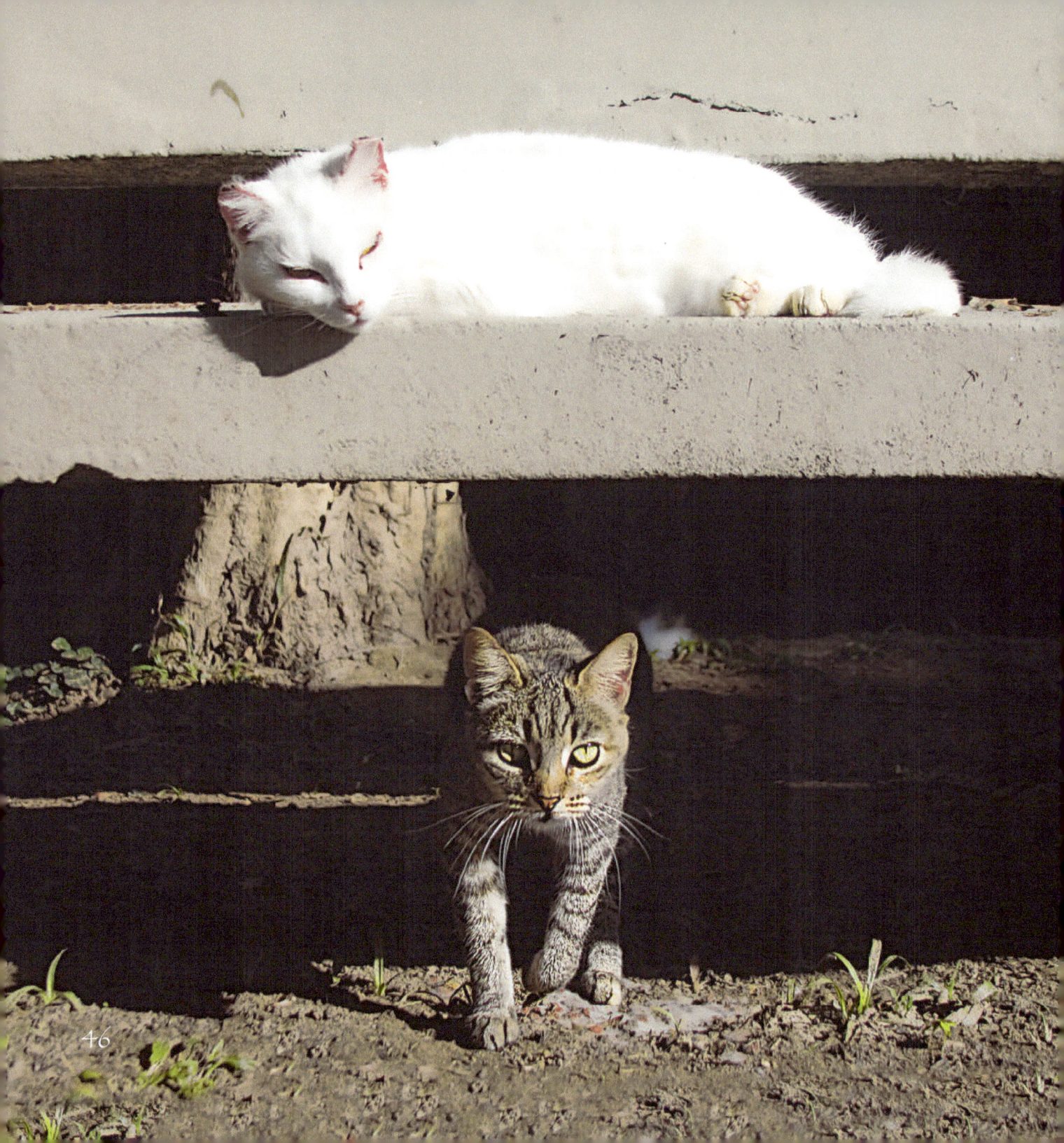

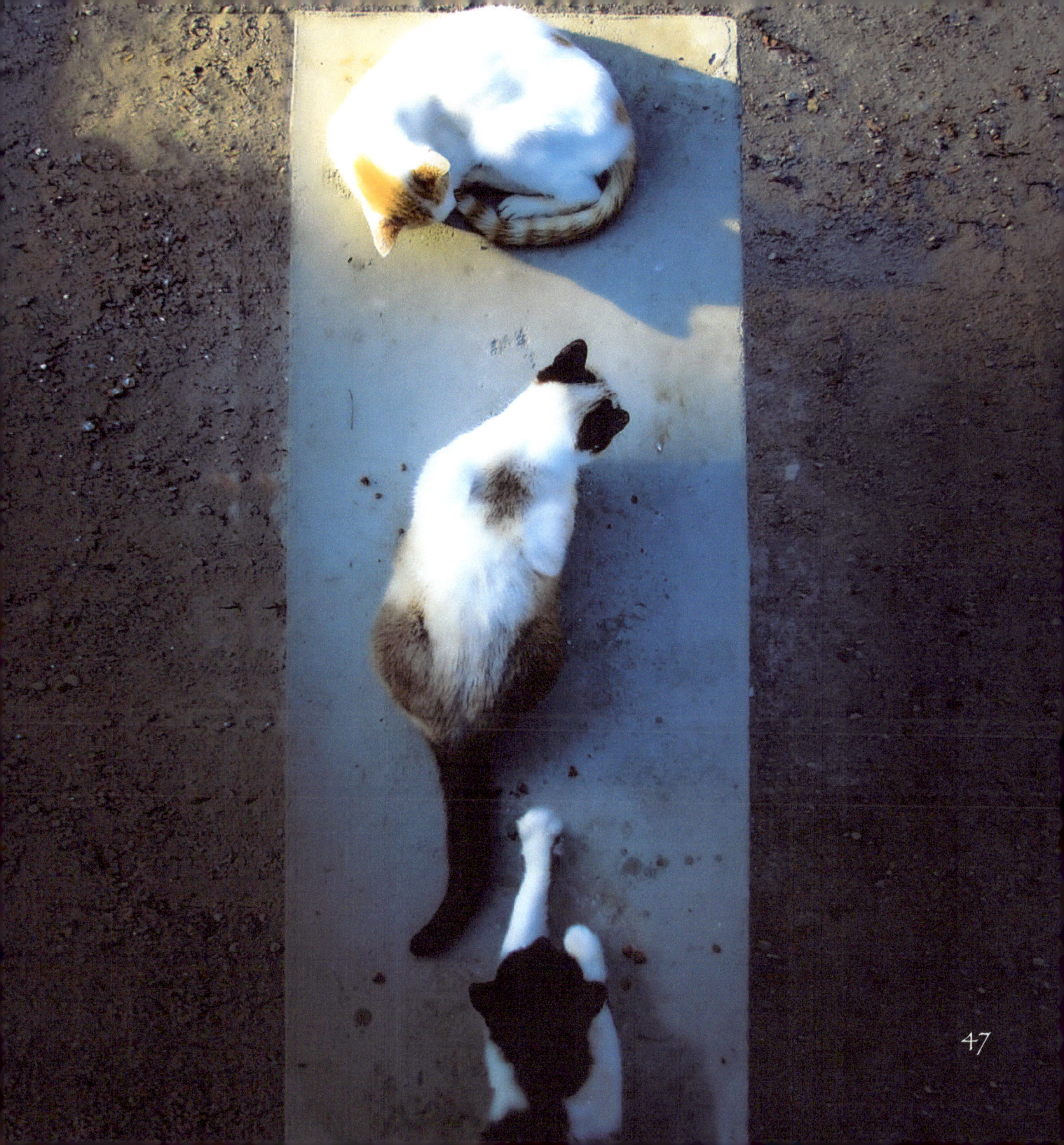

When a cat's eyes first open they are always blue

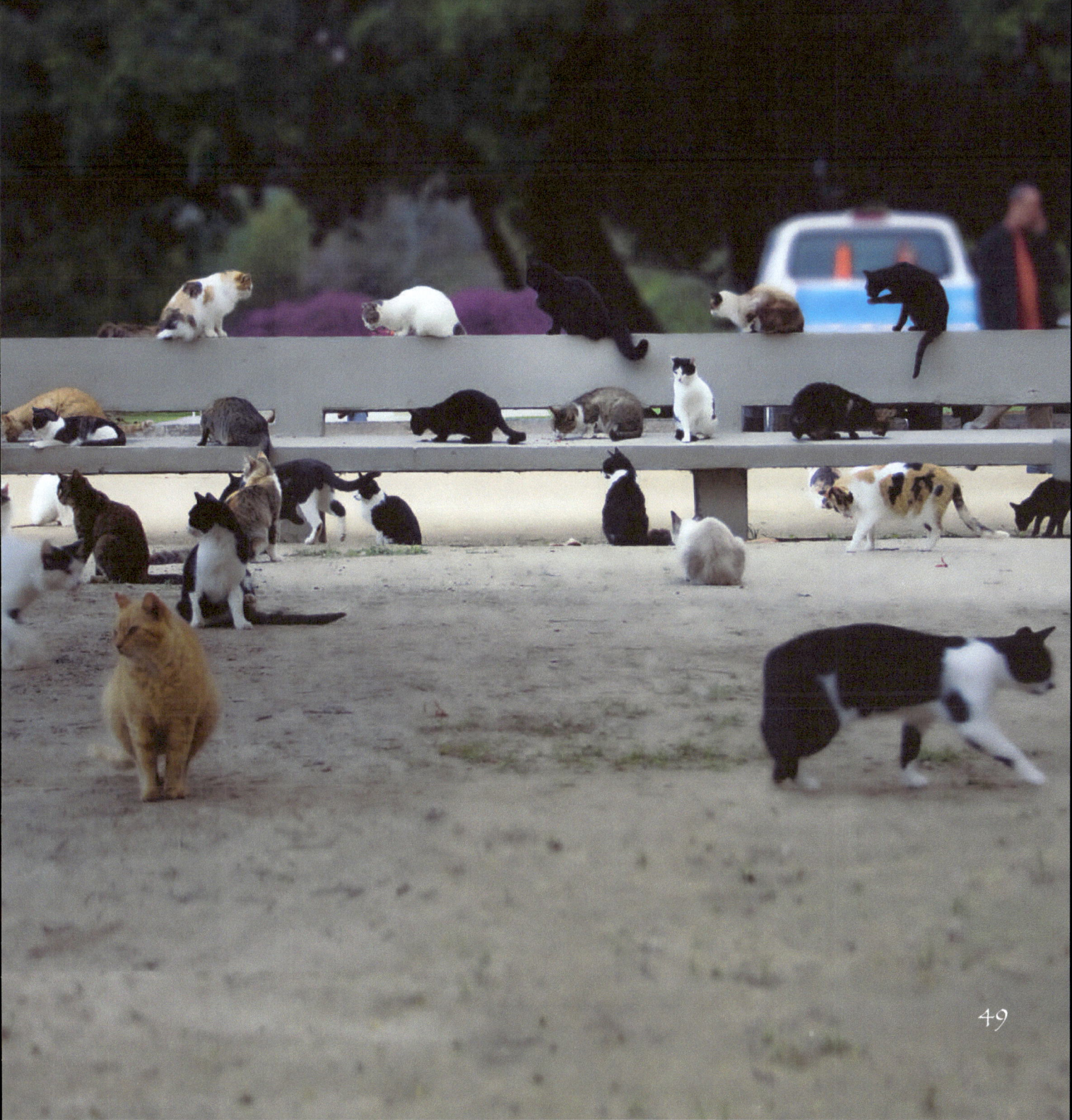

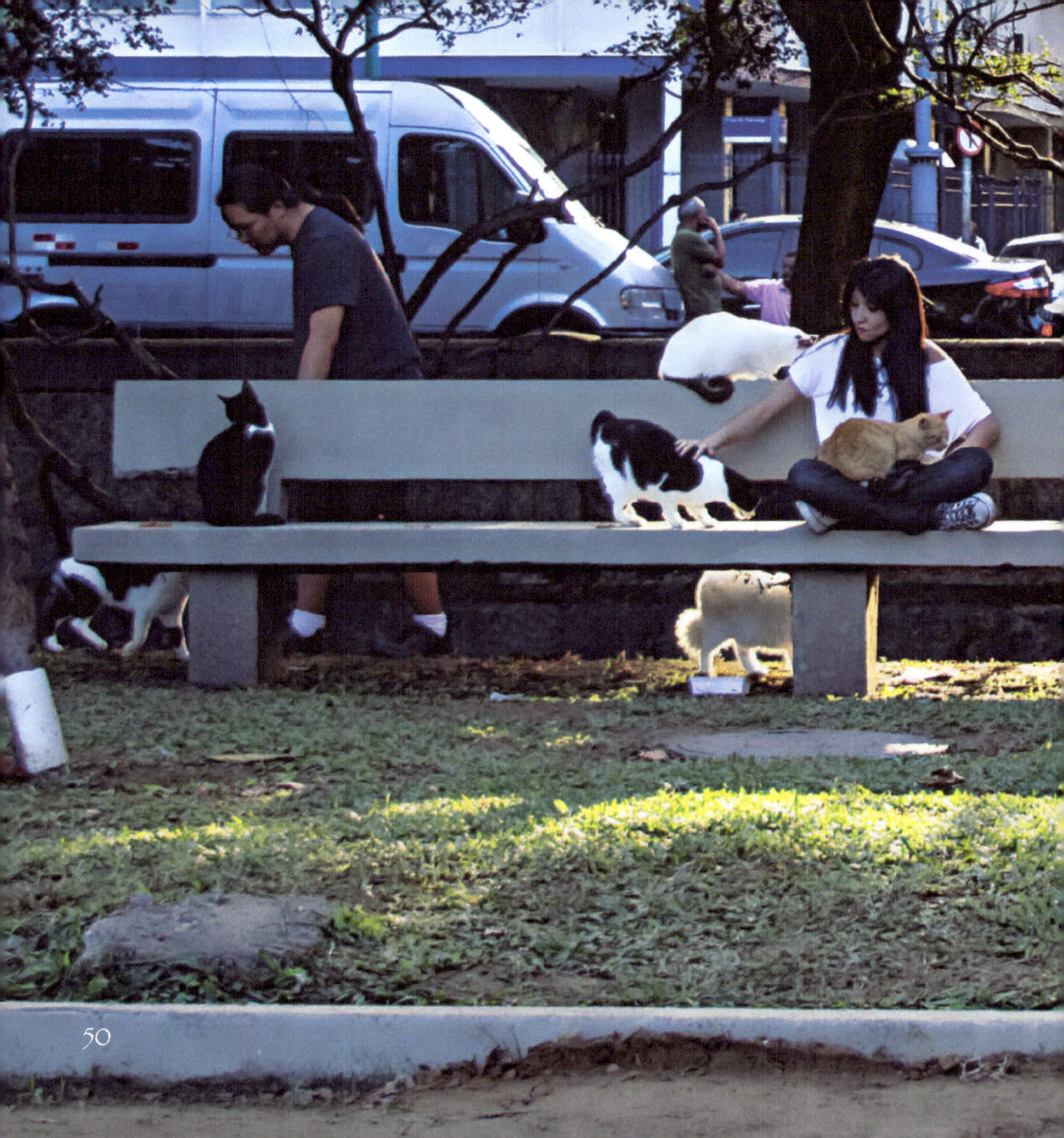

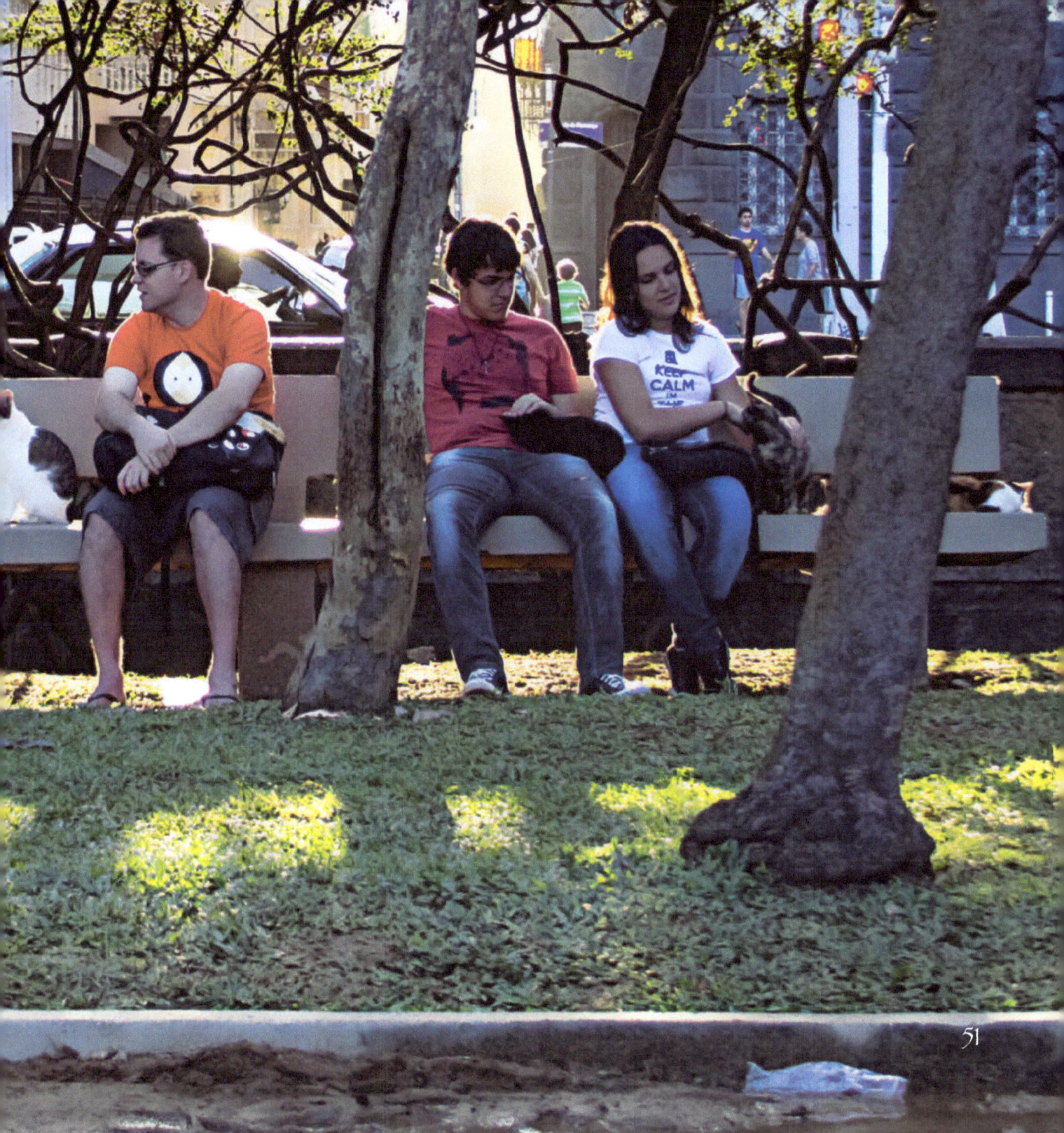

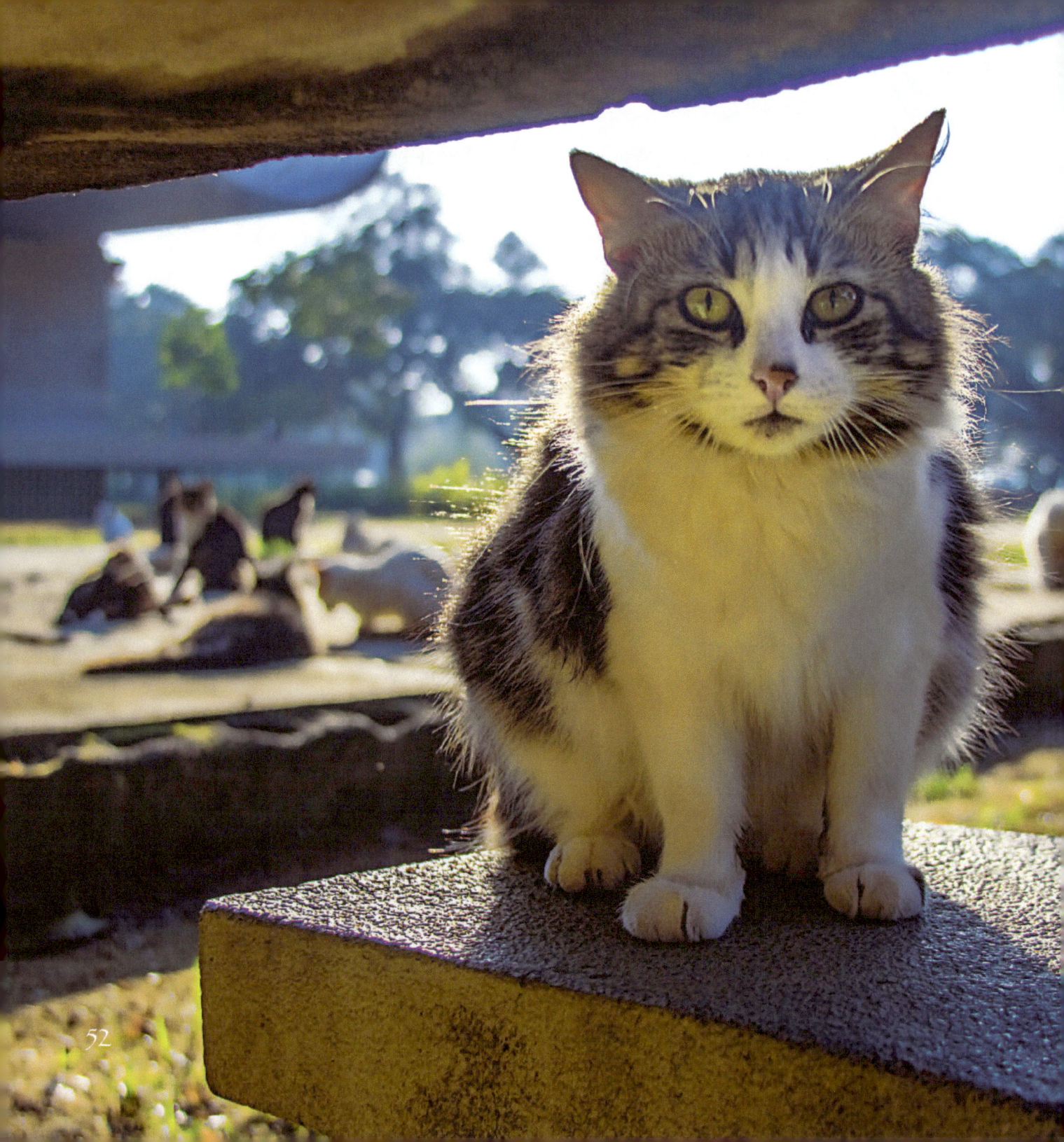

In January 1502 Portuguese explorer Gaspar de Lemos entered Brazil's Guanabara Bay and named the area Rio de Janeiro meaning "River of January"

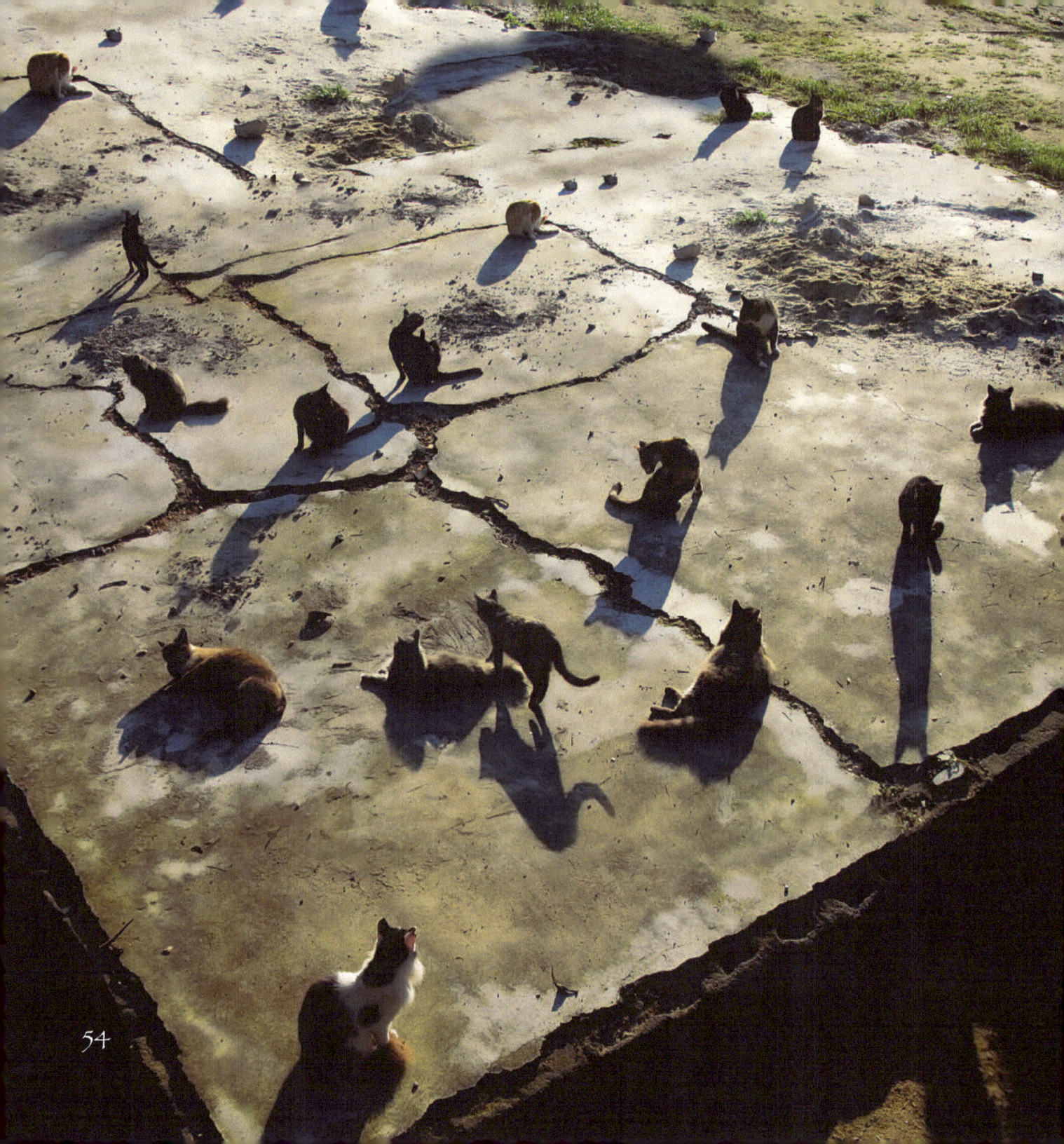

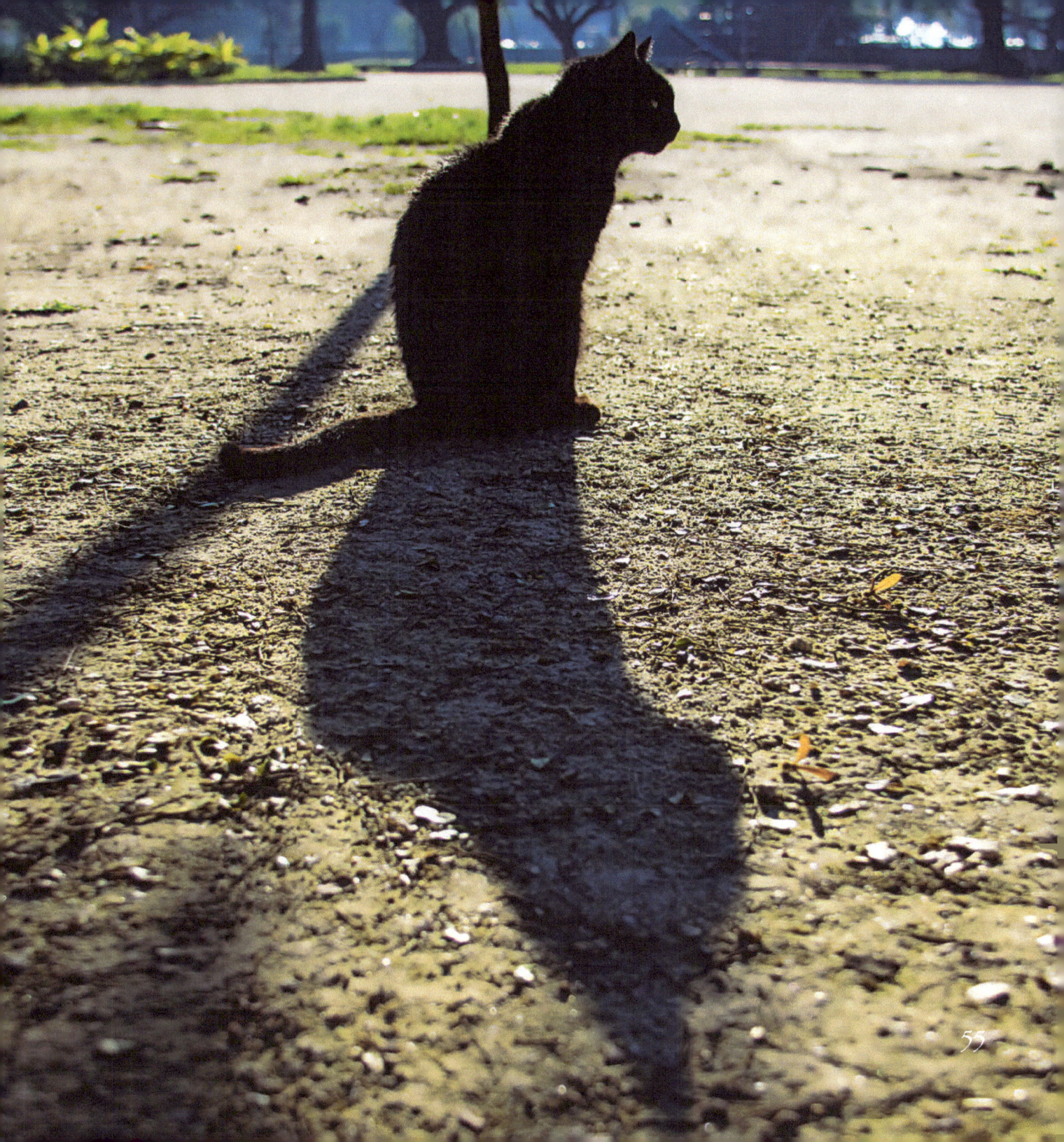

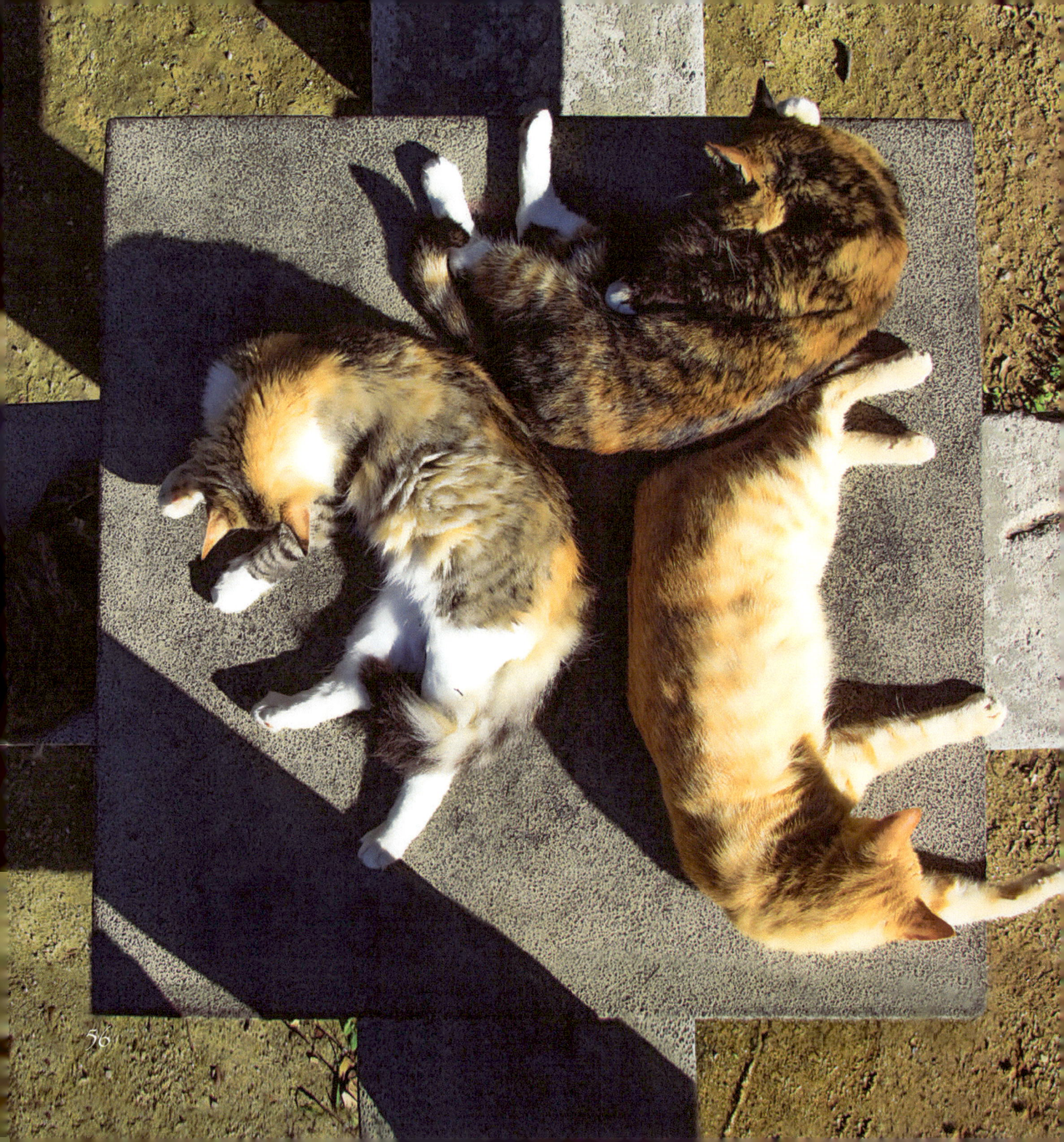

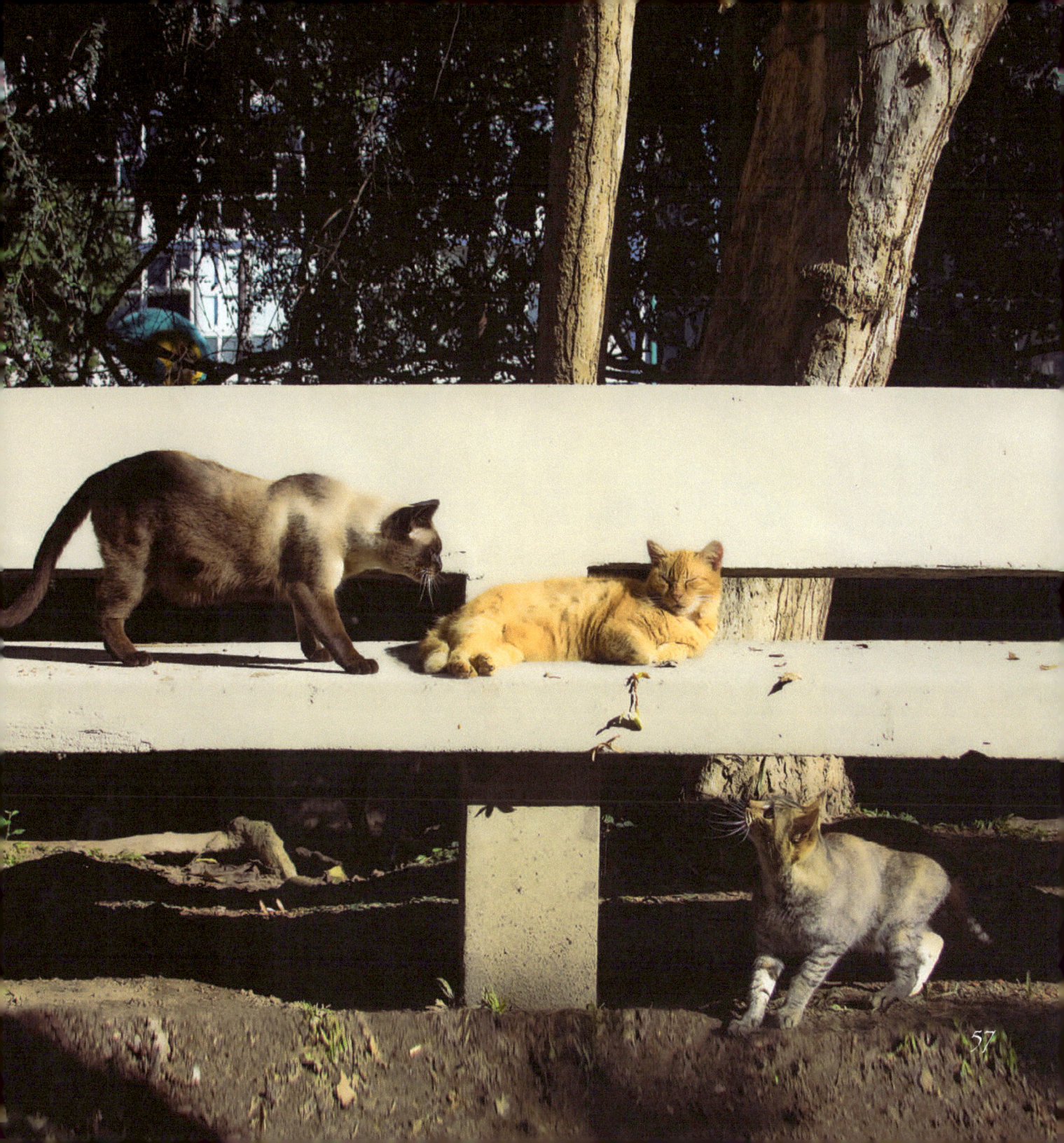

A cat can jump up to seven times it height

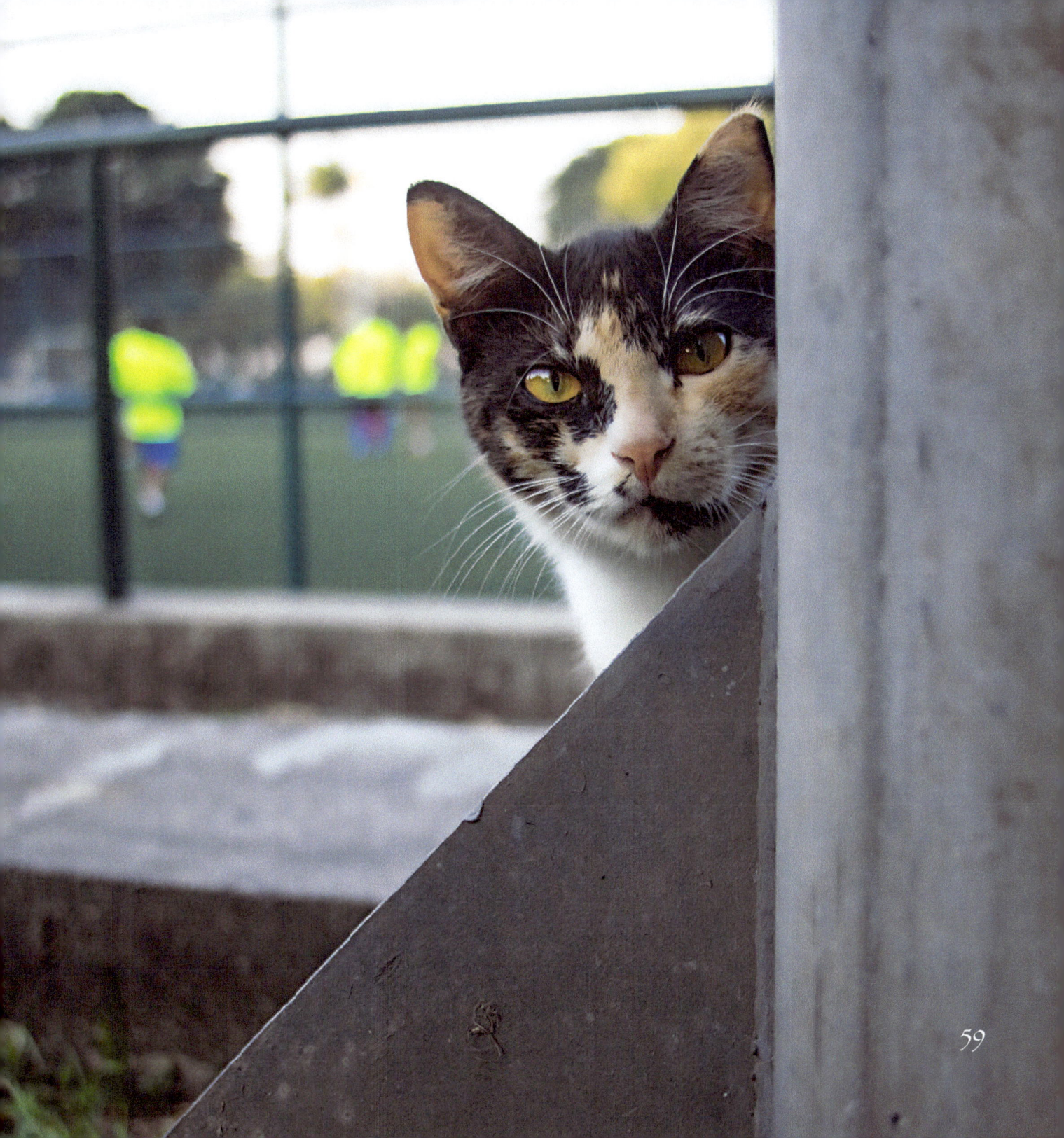

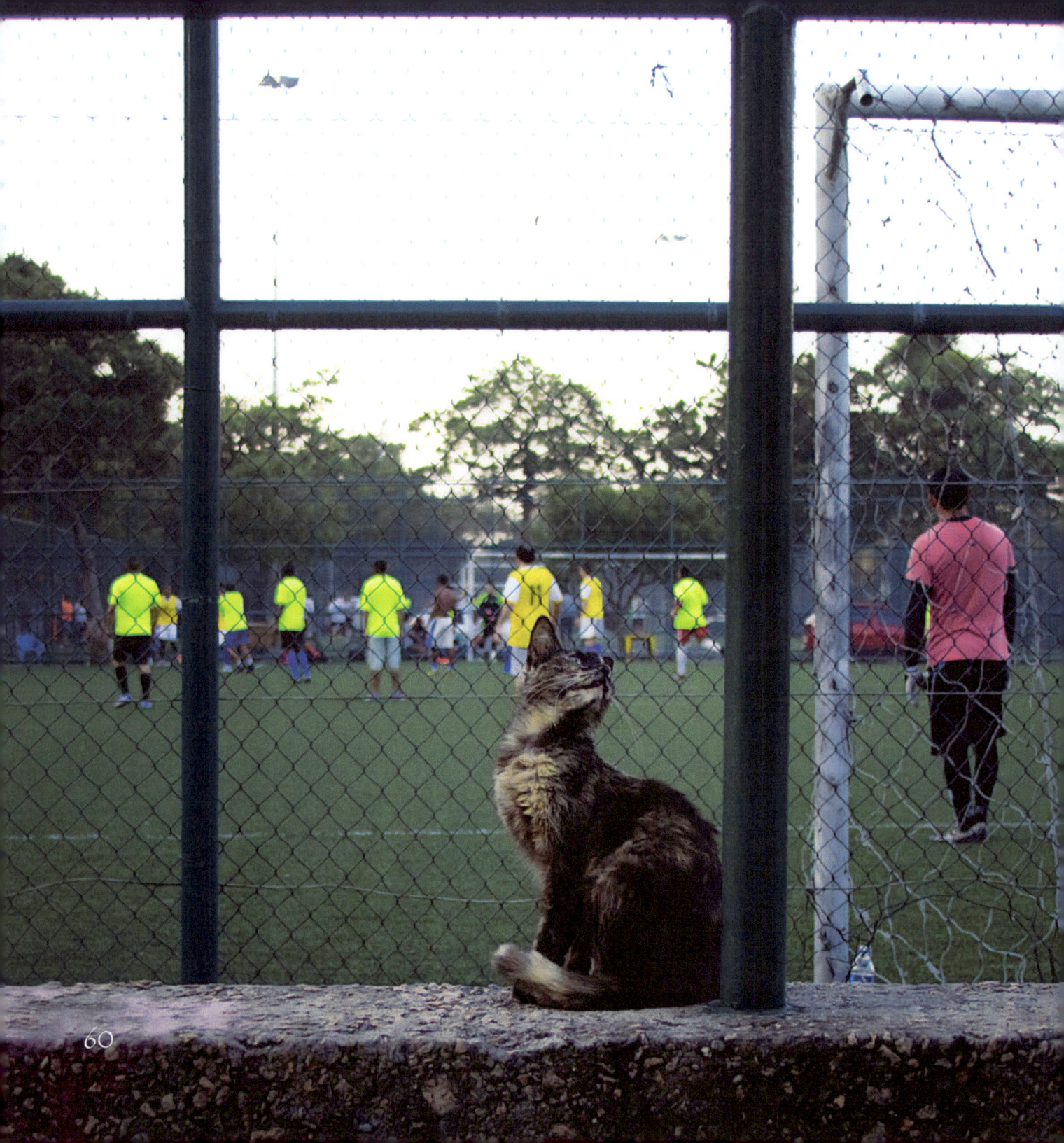

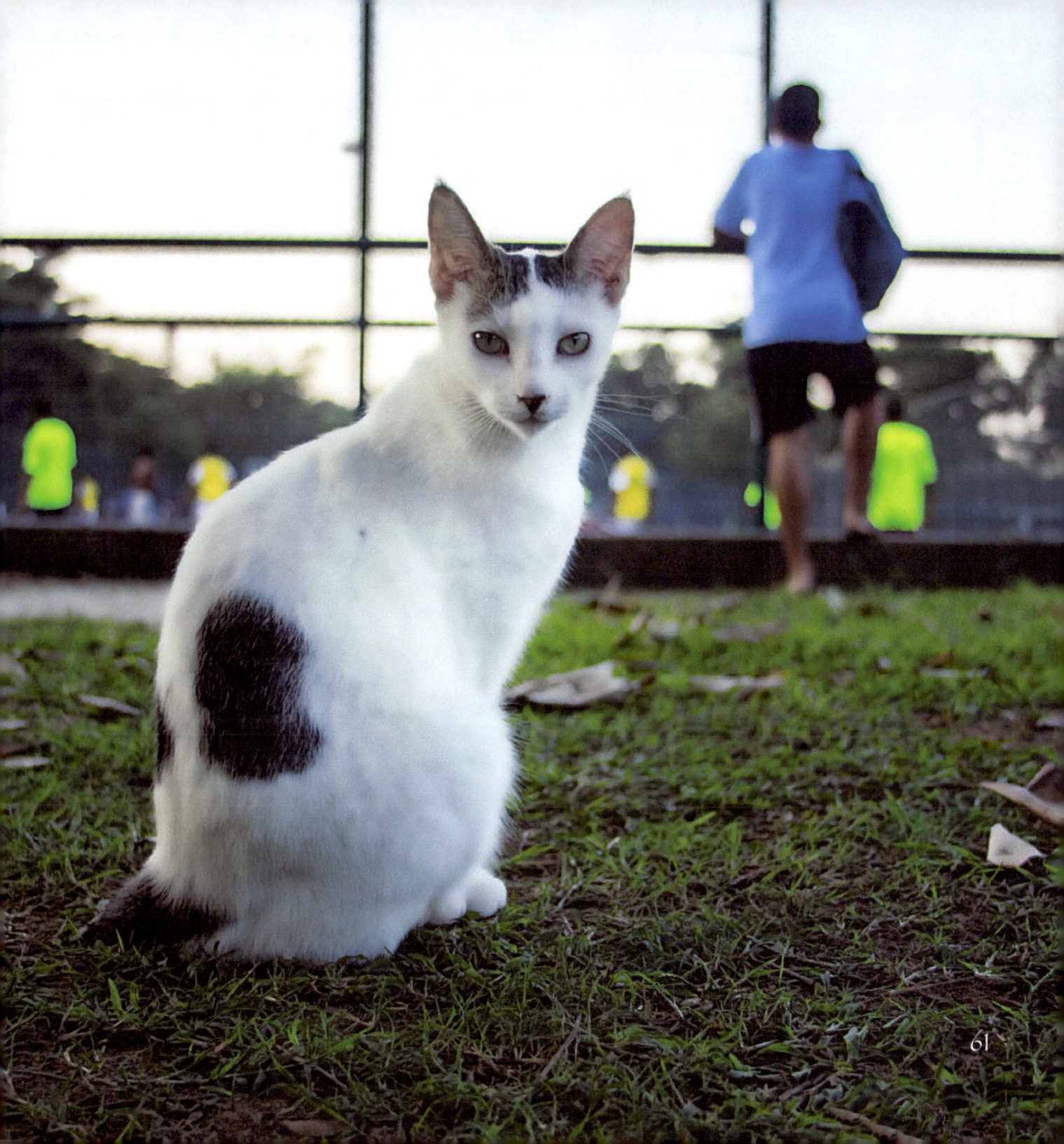

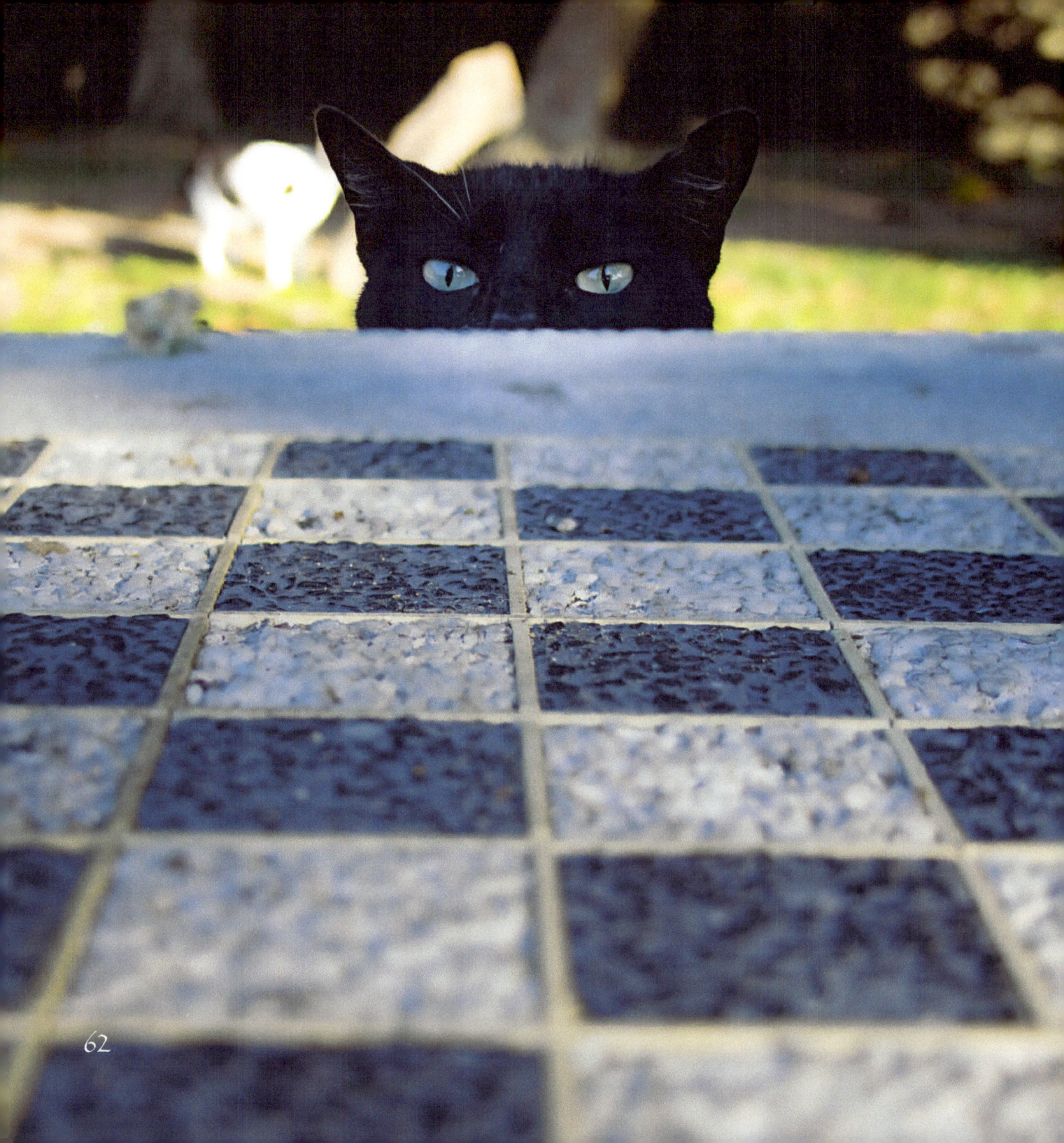

Rio's beloved 98-foot statue, Christ the Redeemer, was completed in 1931 and is one of the 7 Wonders of the World

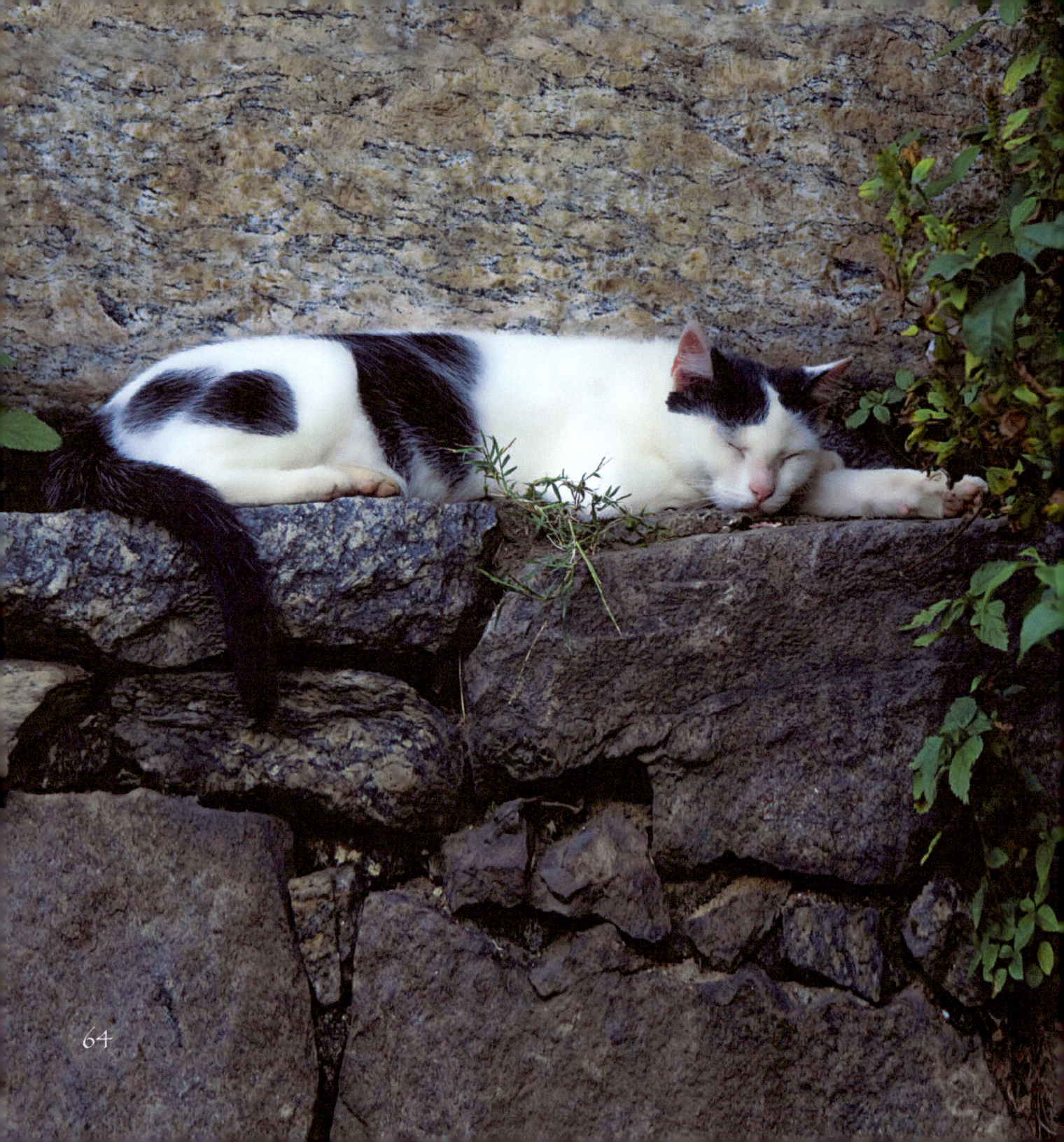

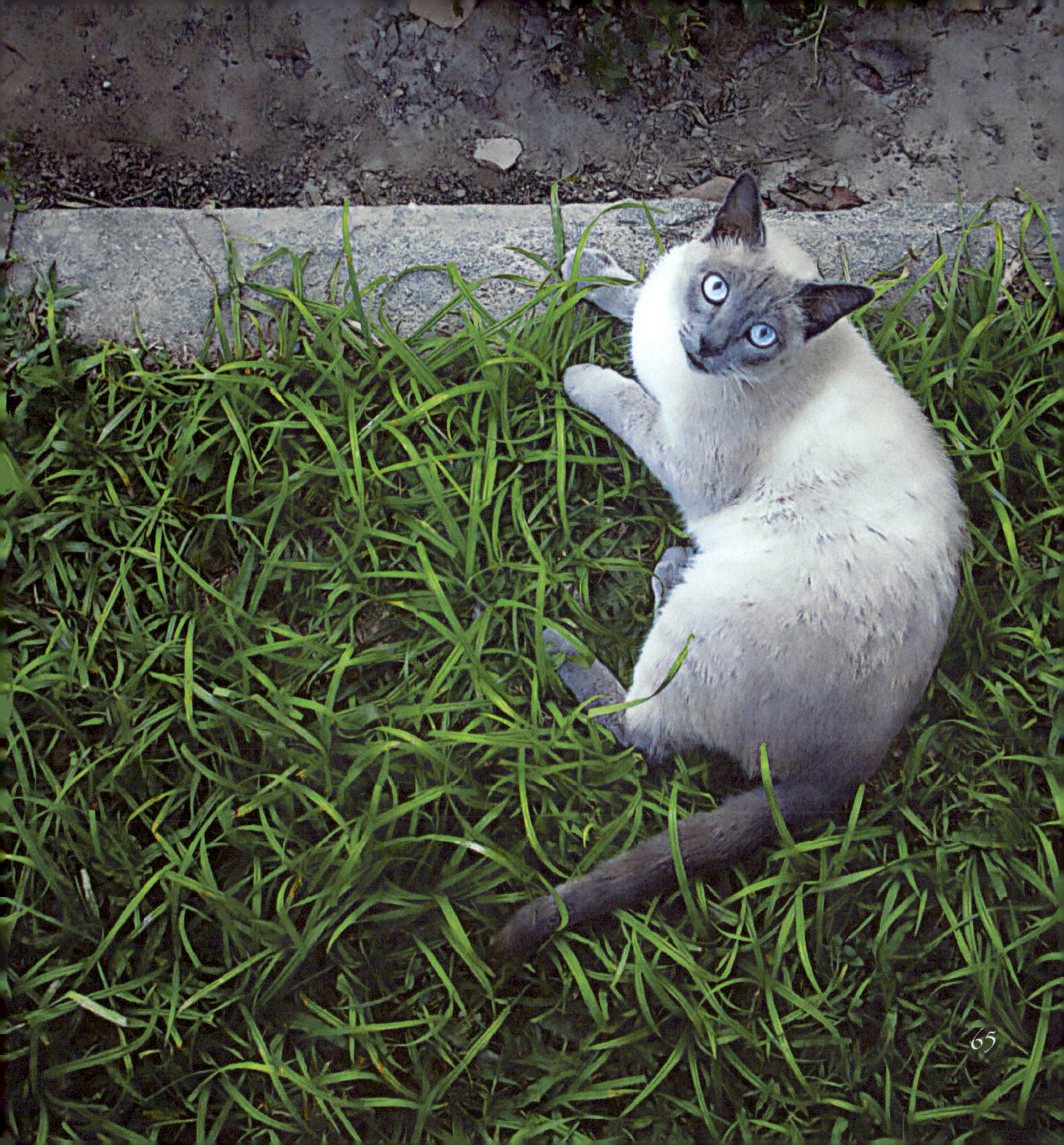

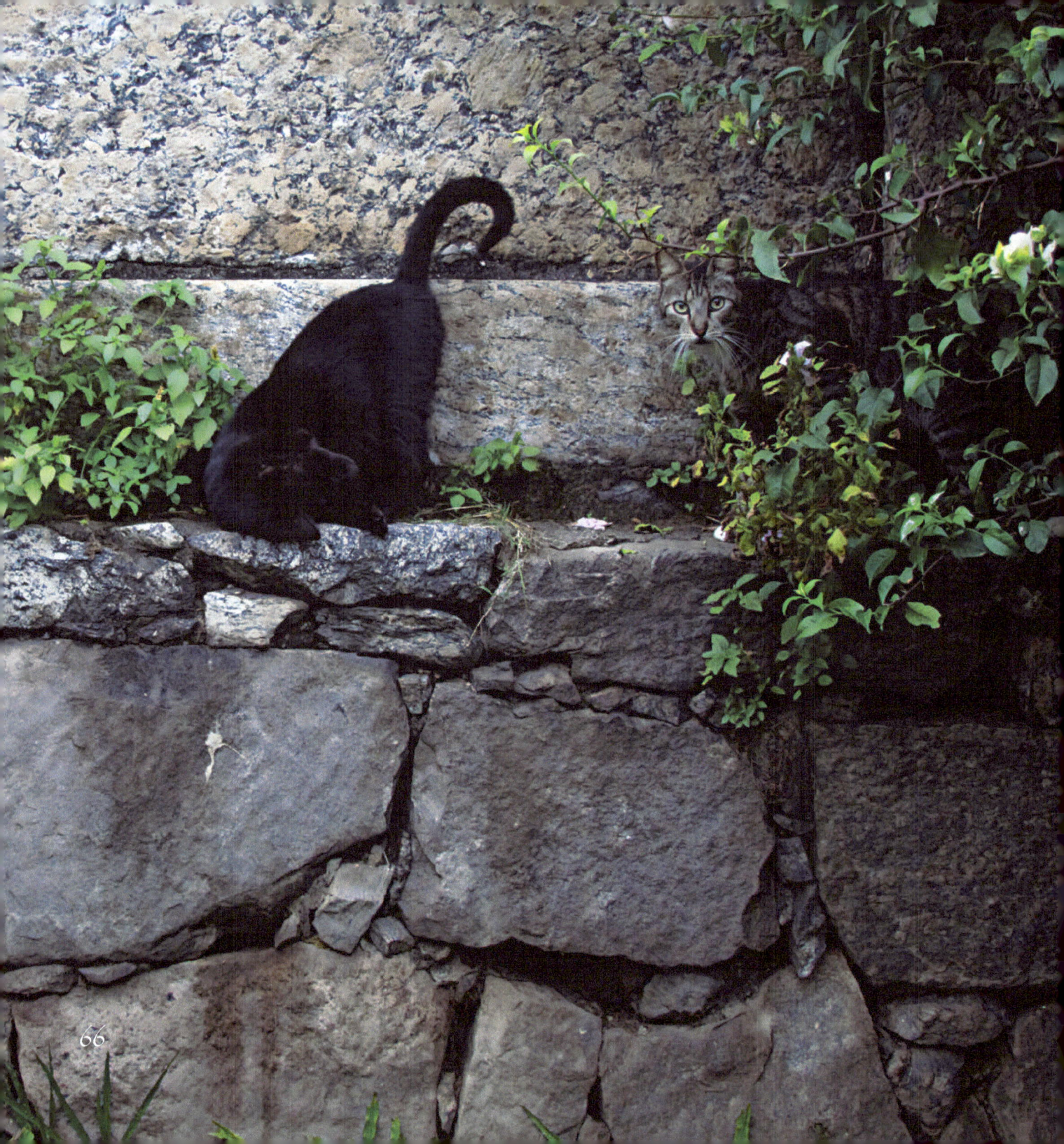

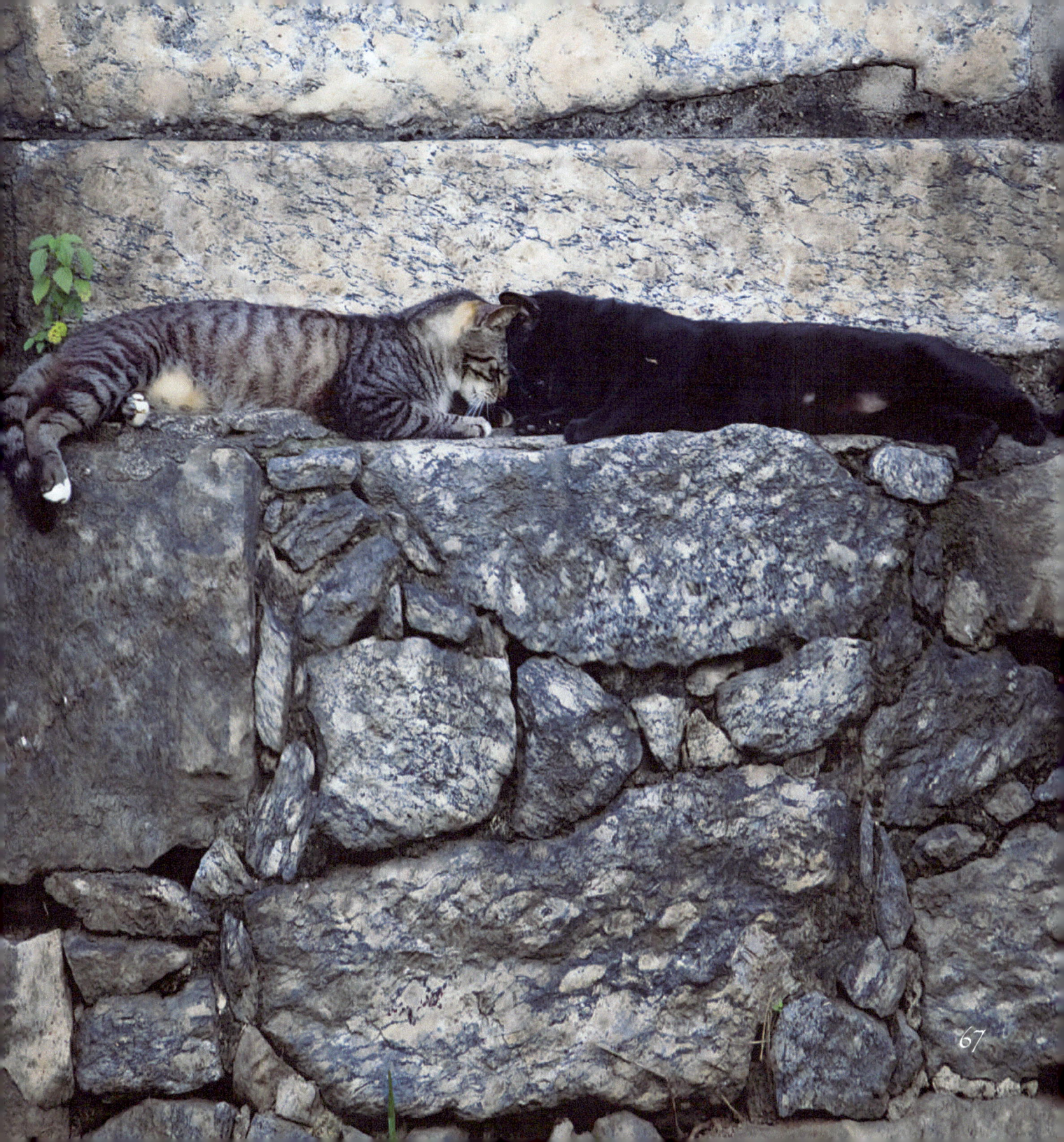

The cat's front paw has 5 toes and the back paws have 4

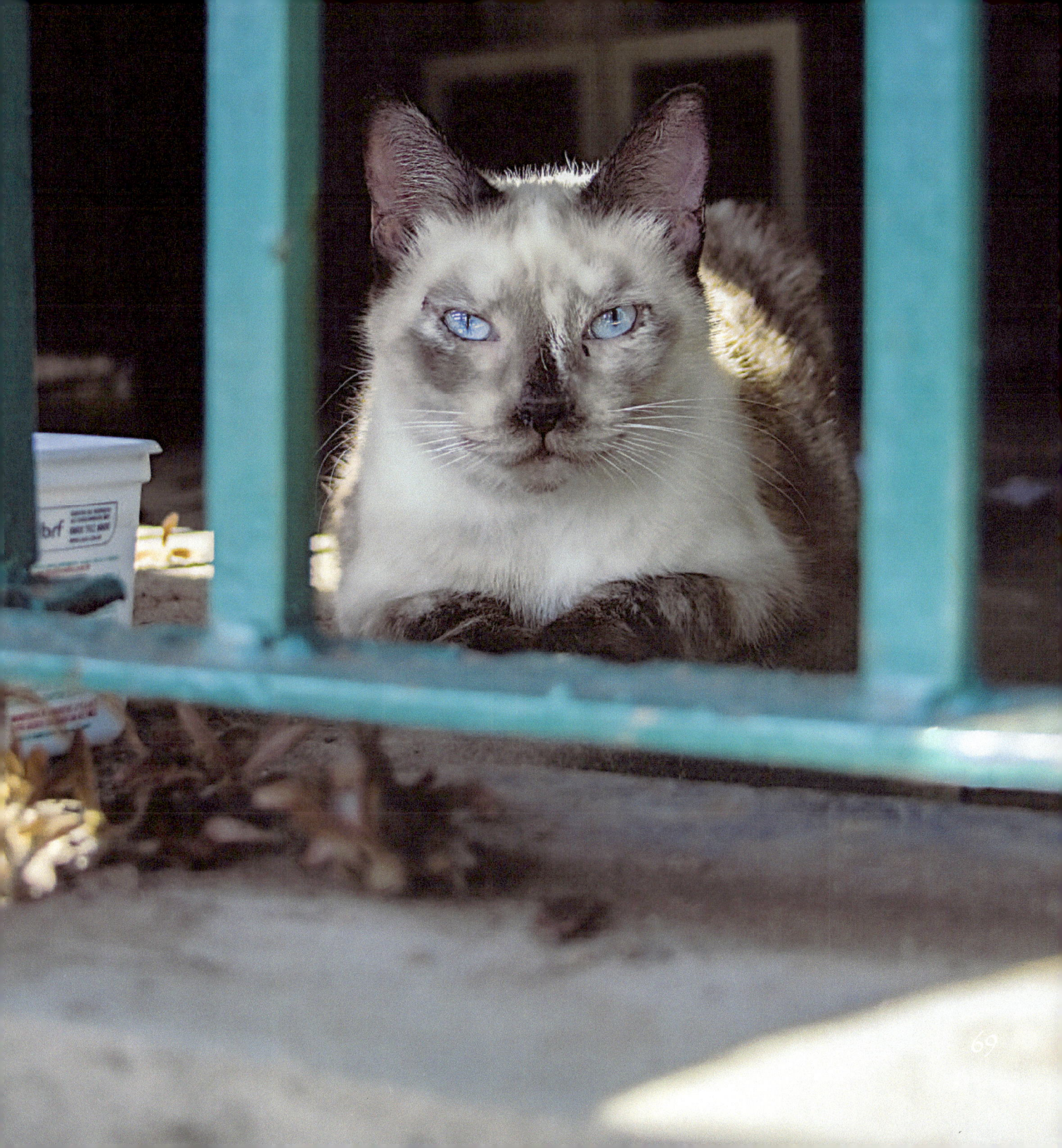

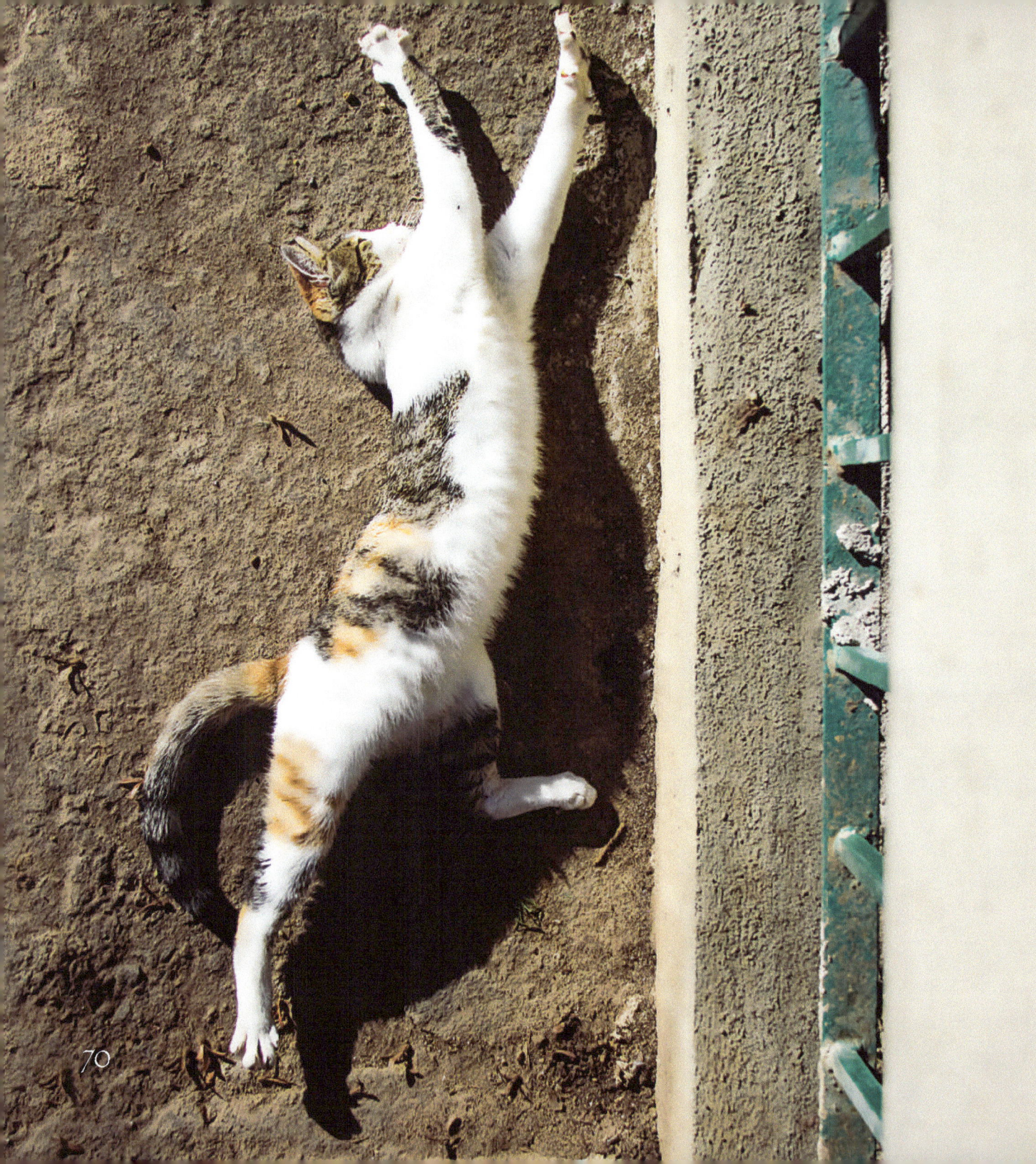

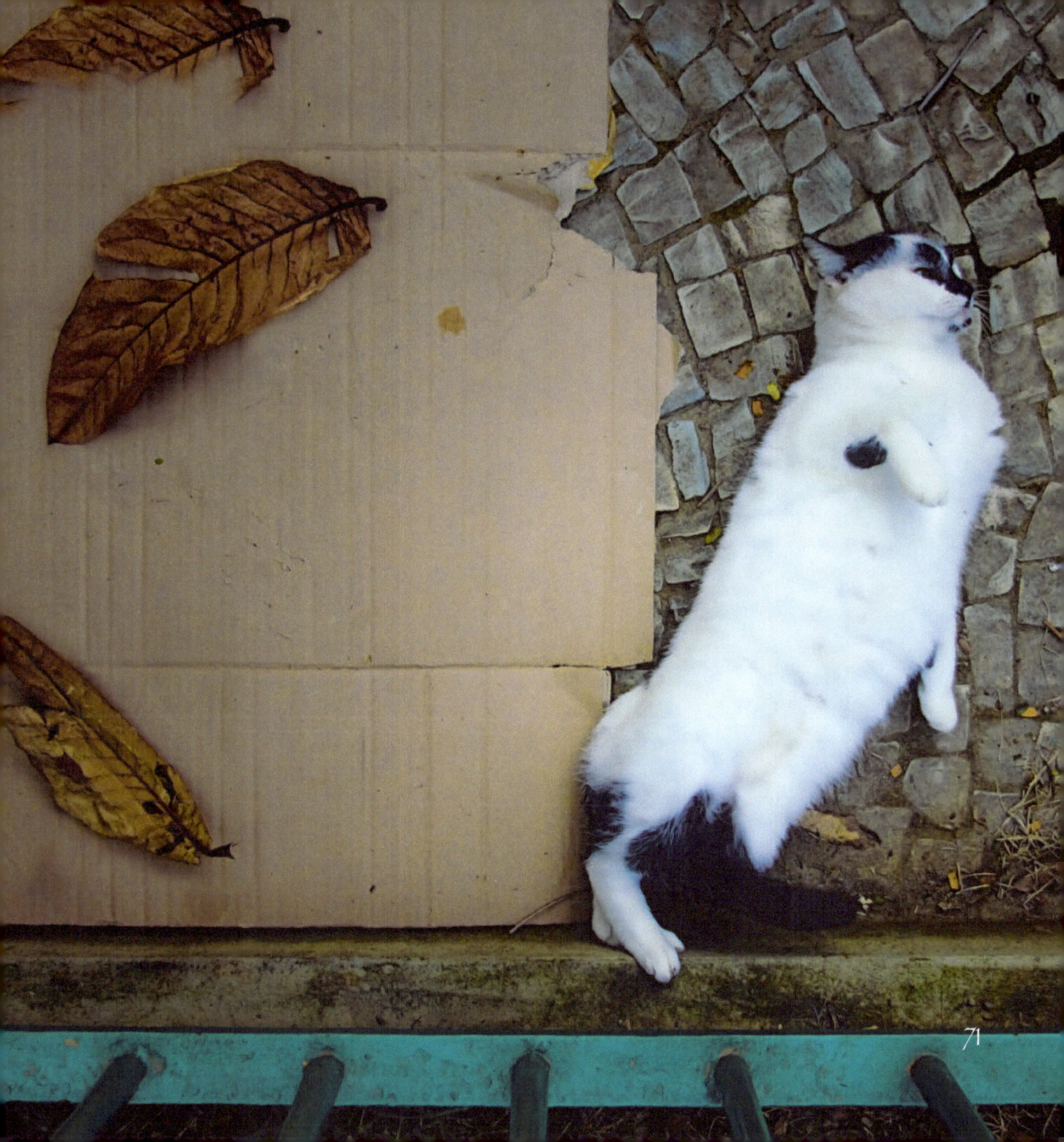

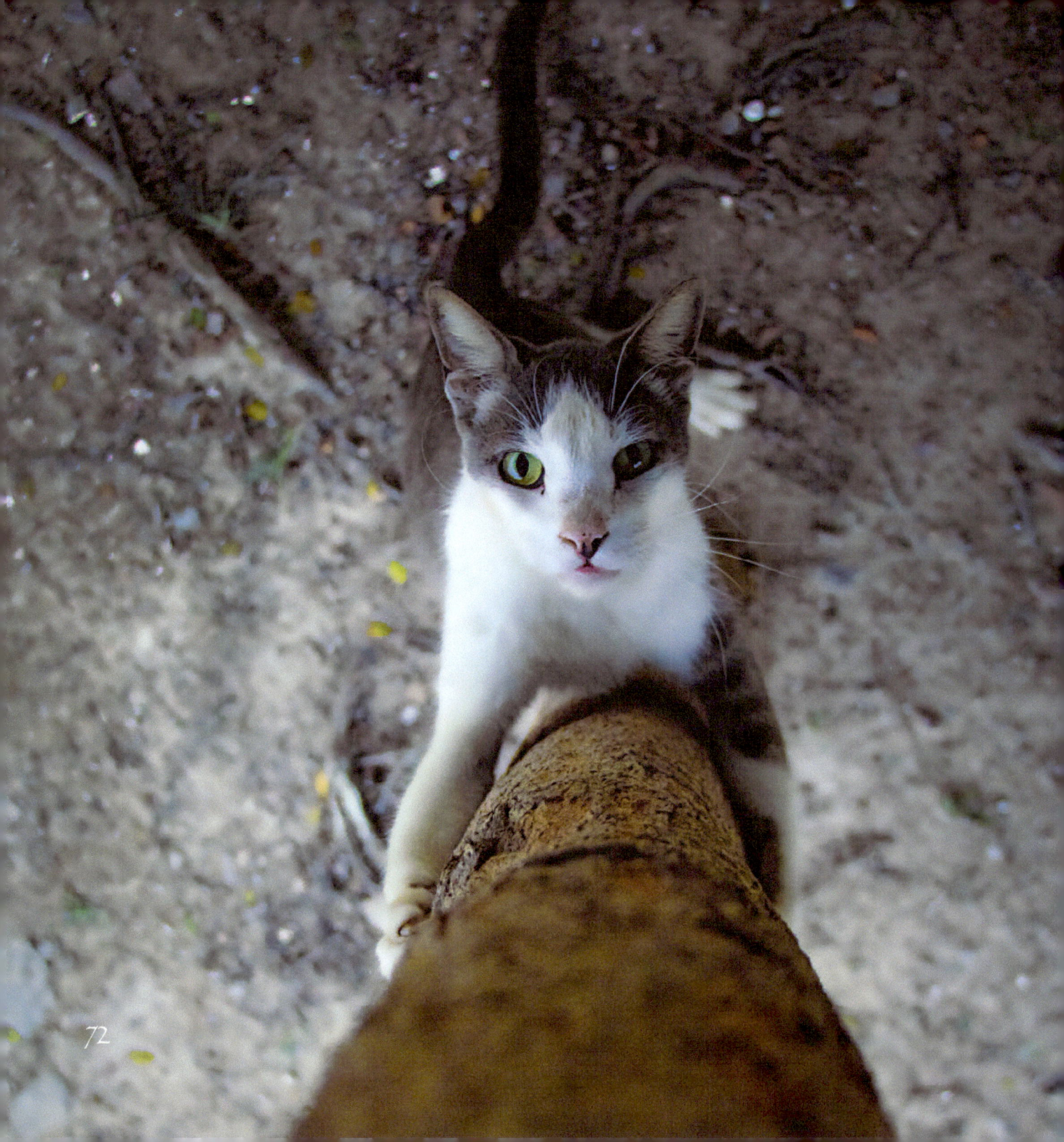

Brazil has the world's largest beach at 24,606 feet long

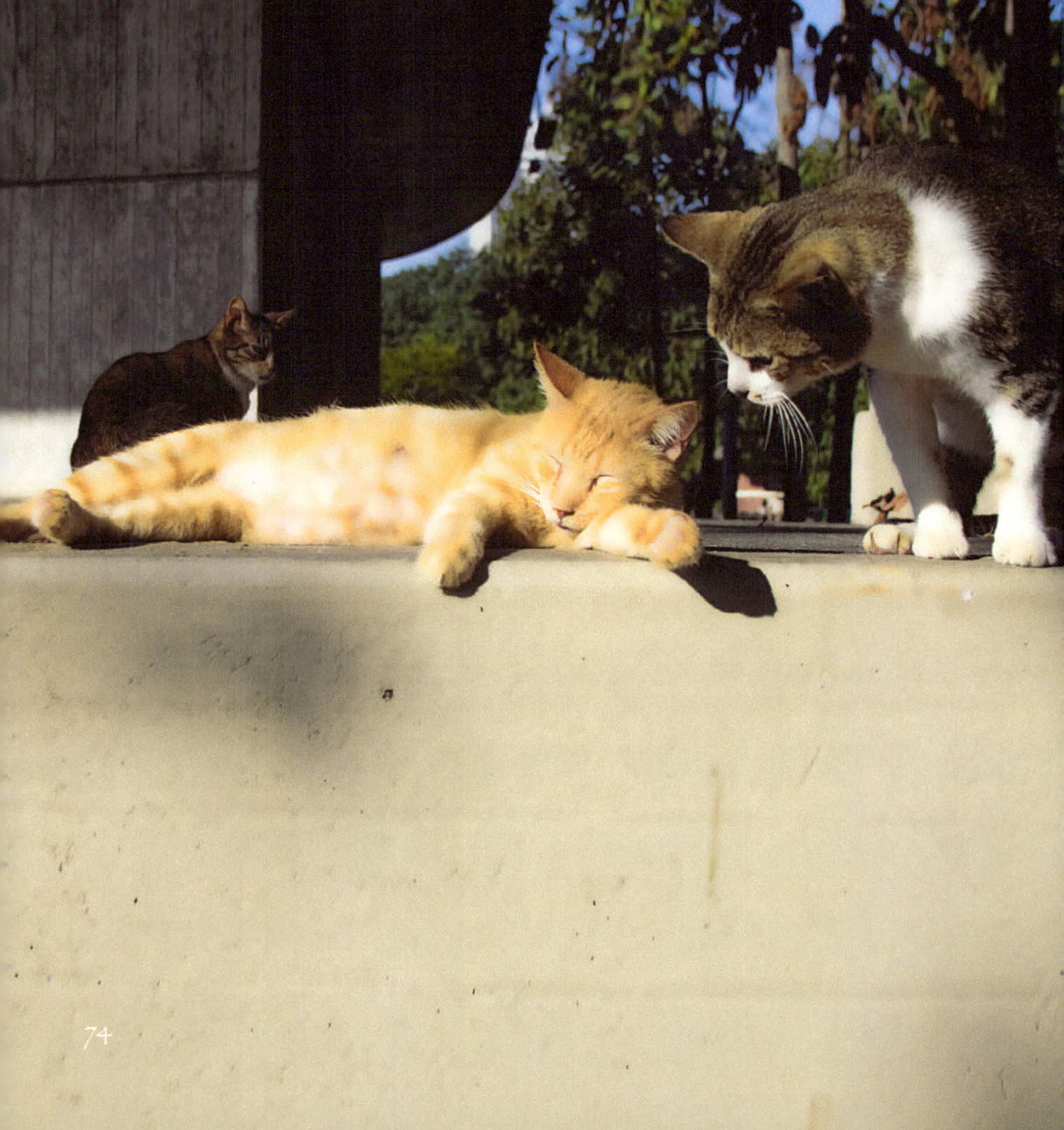

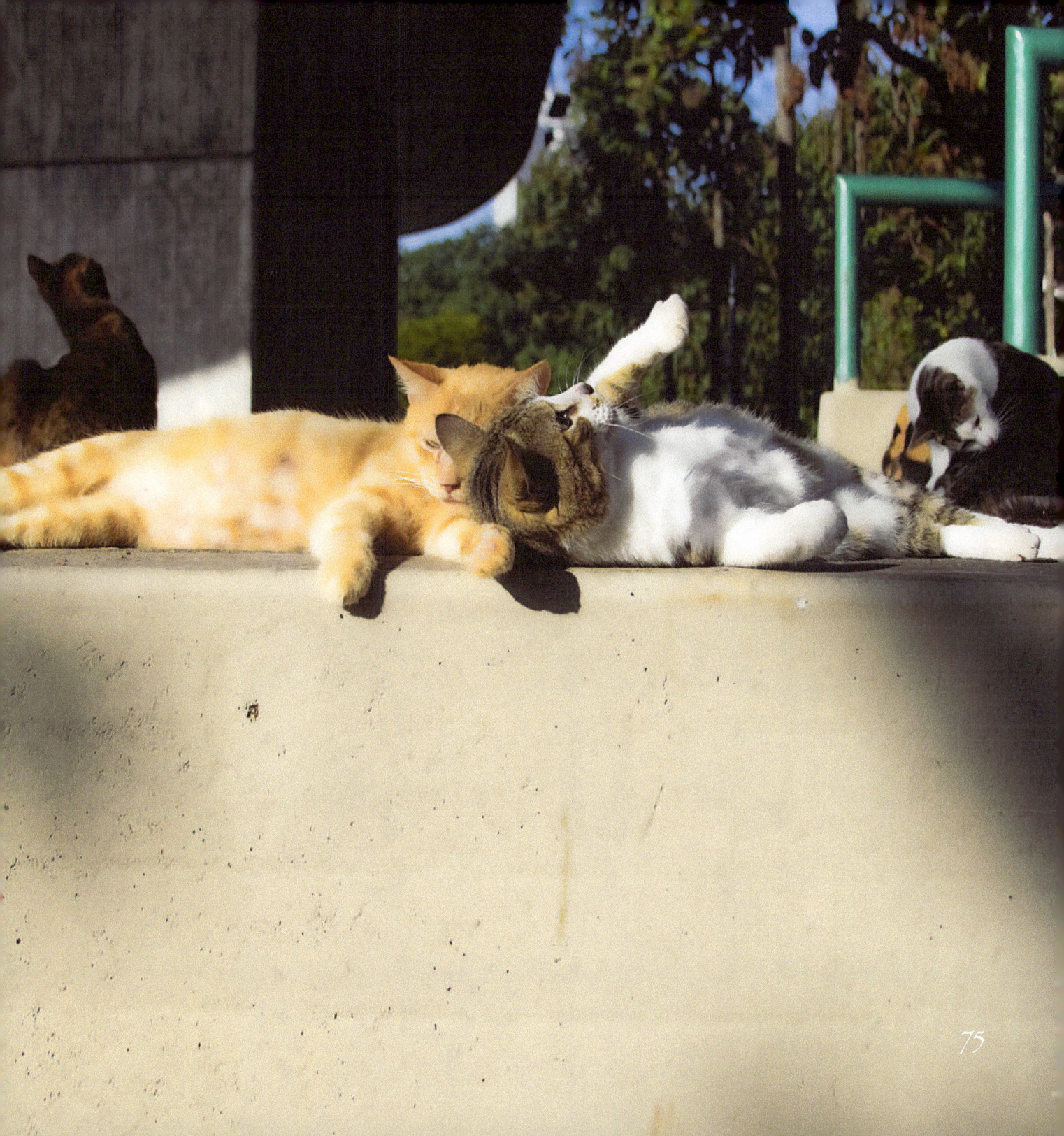

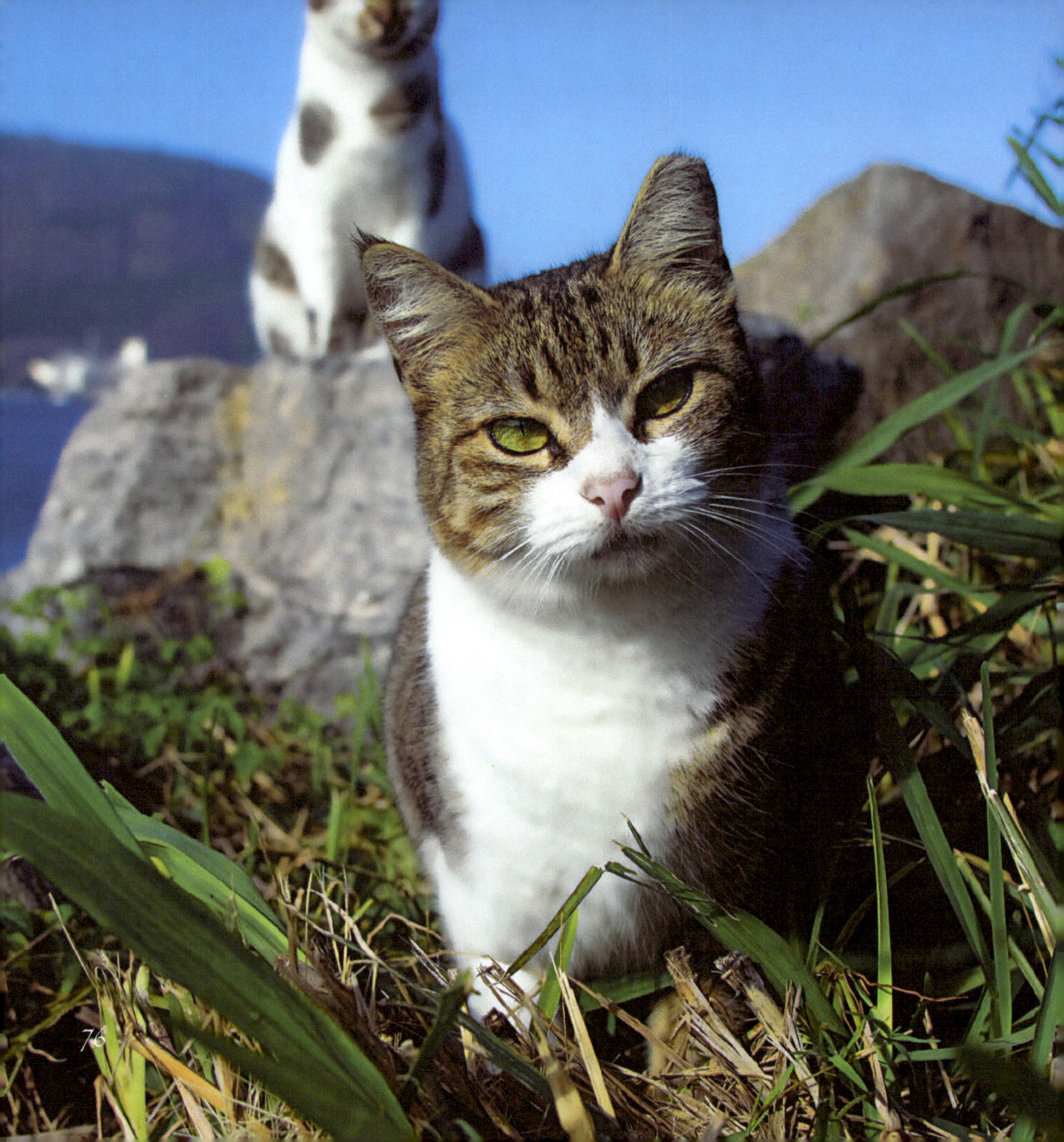

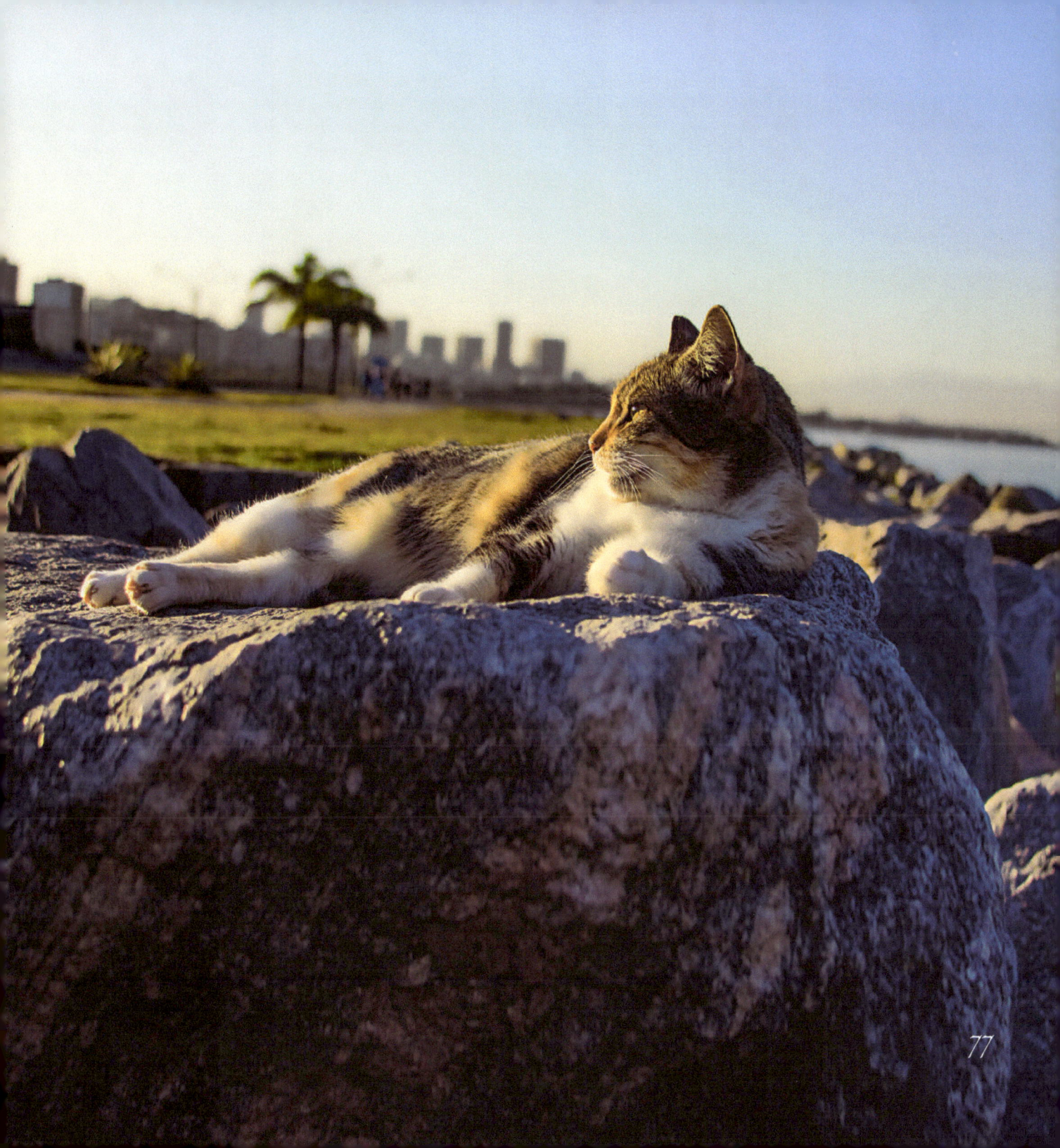

The smallest wildcat today is the Black-footed cat the females are less than 20 inches long and can weigh as little as 2.5 lbs

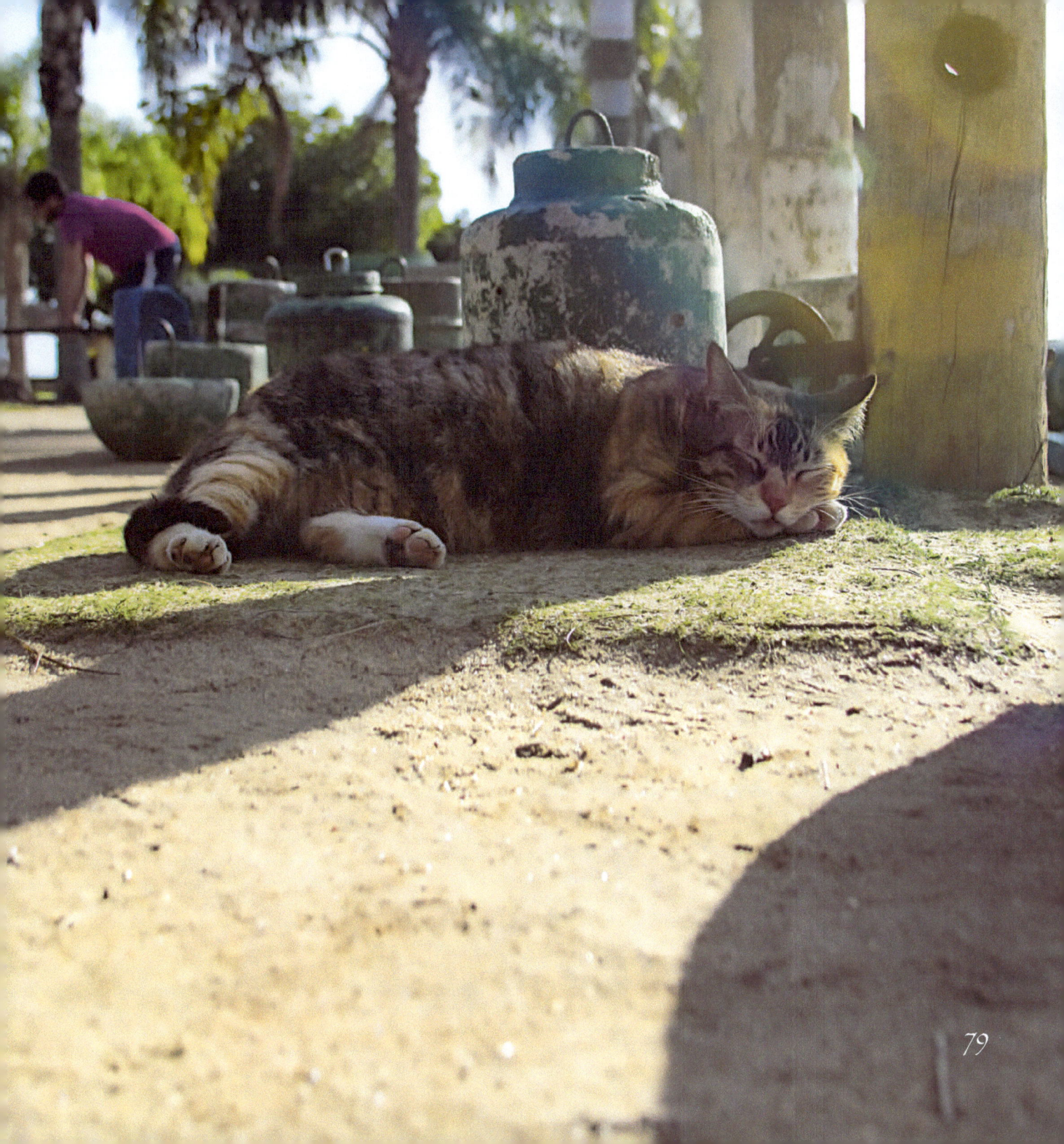

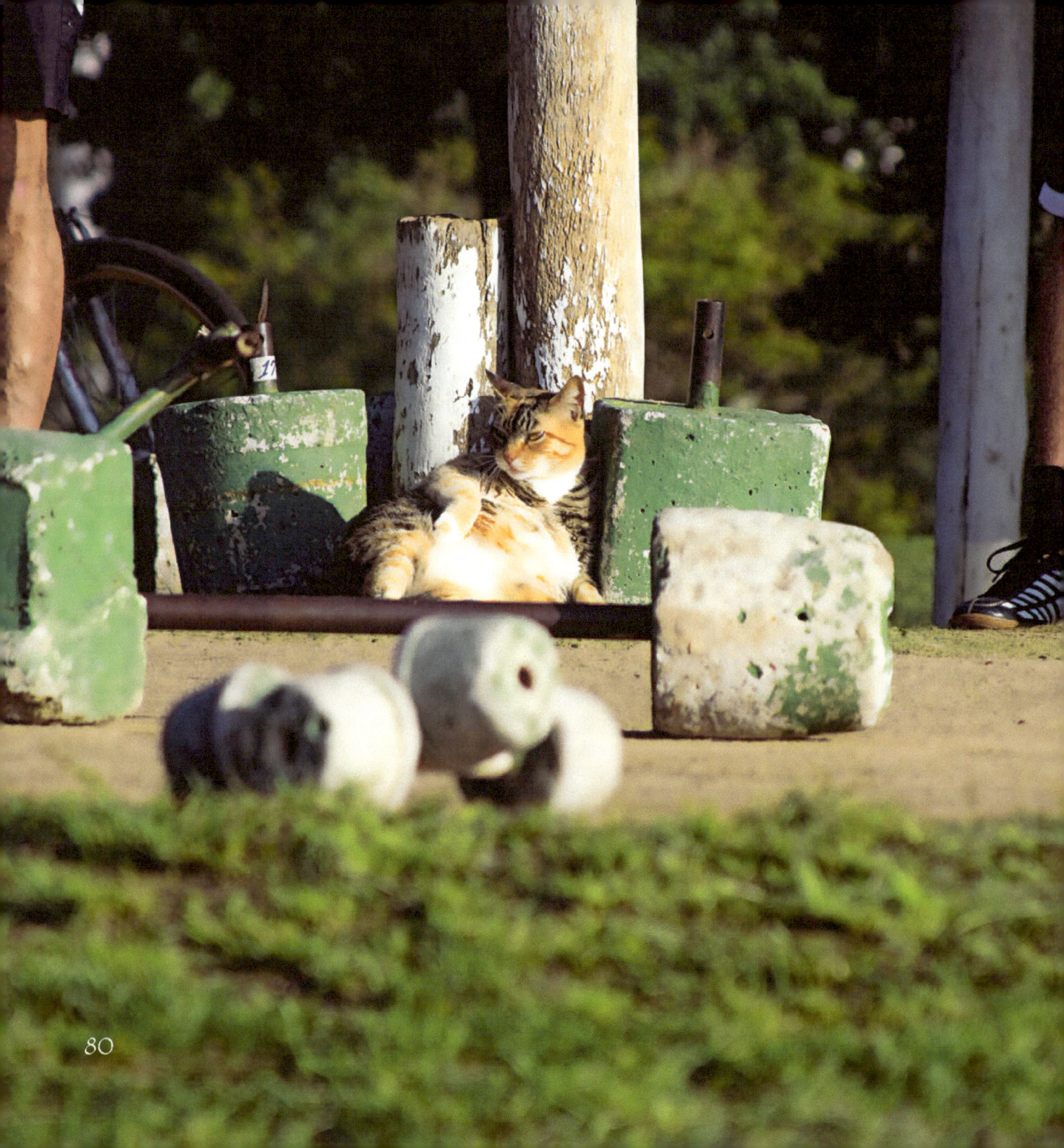

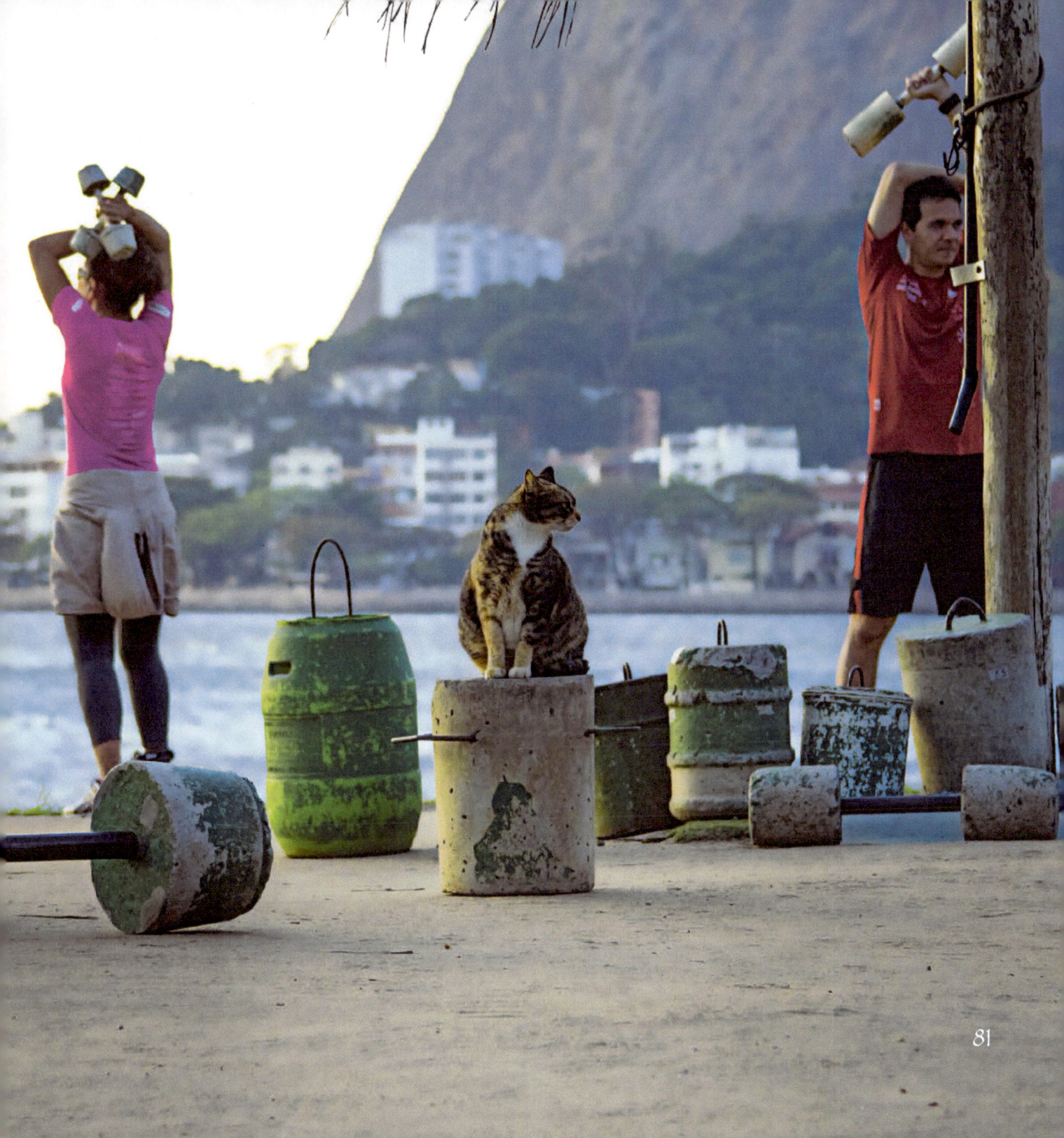

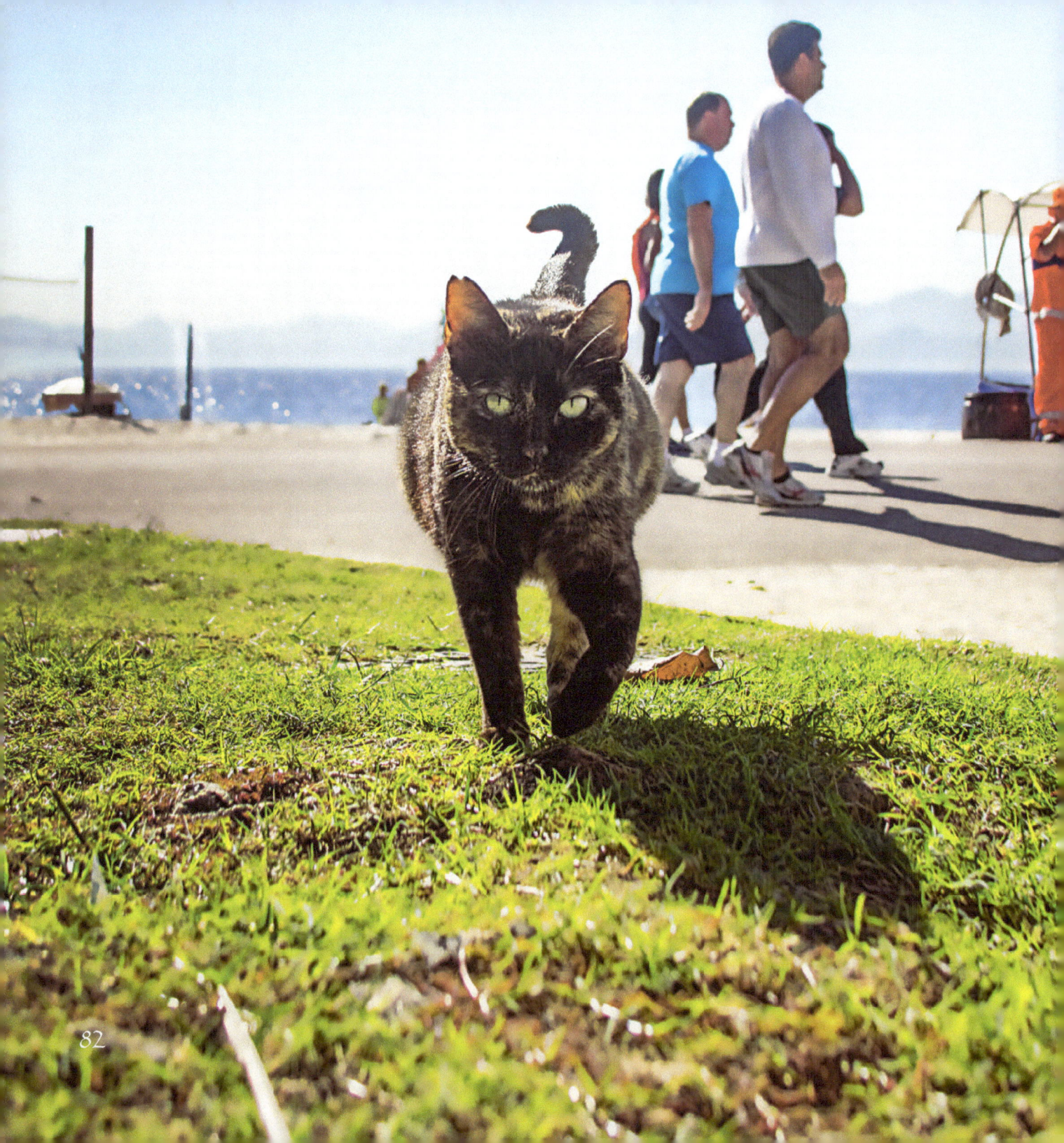

Rio Carnival is the most famous and celebrated carnival festival
in the world with over two million attendees per day

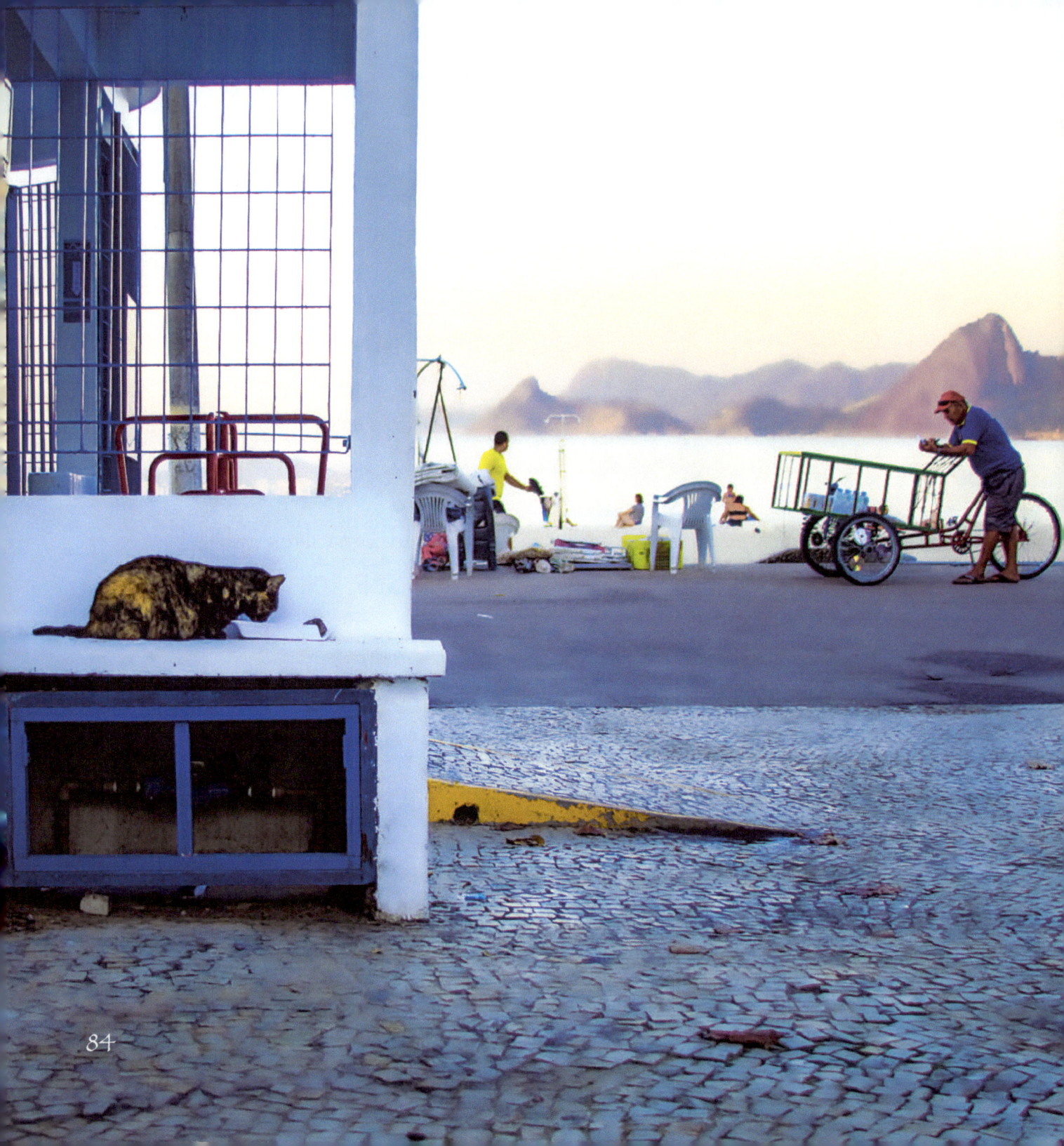

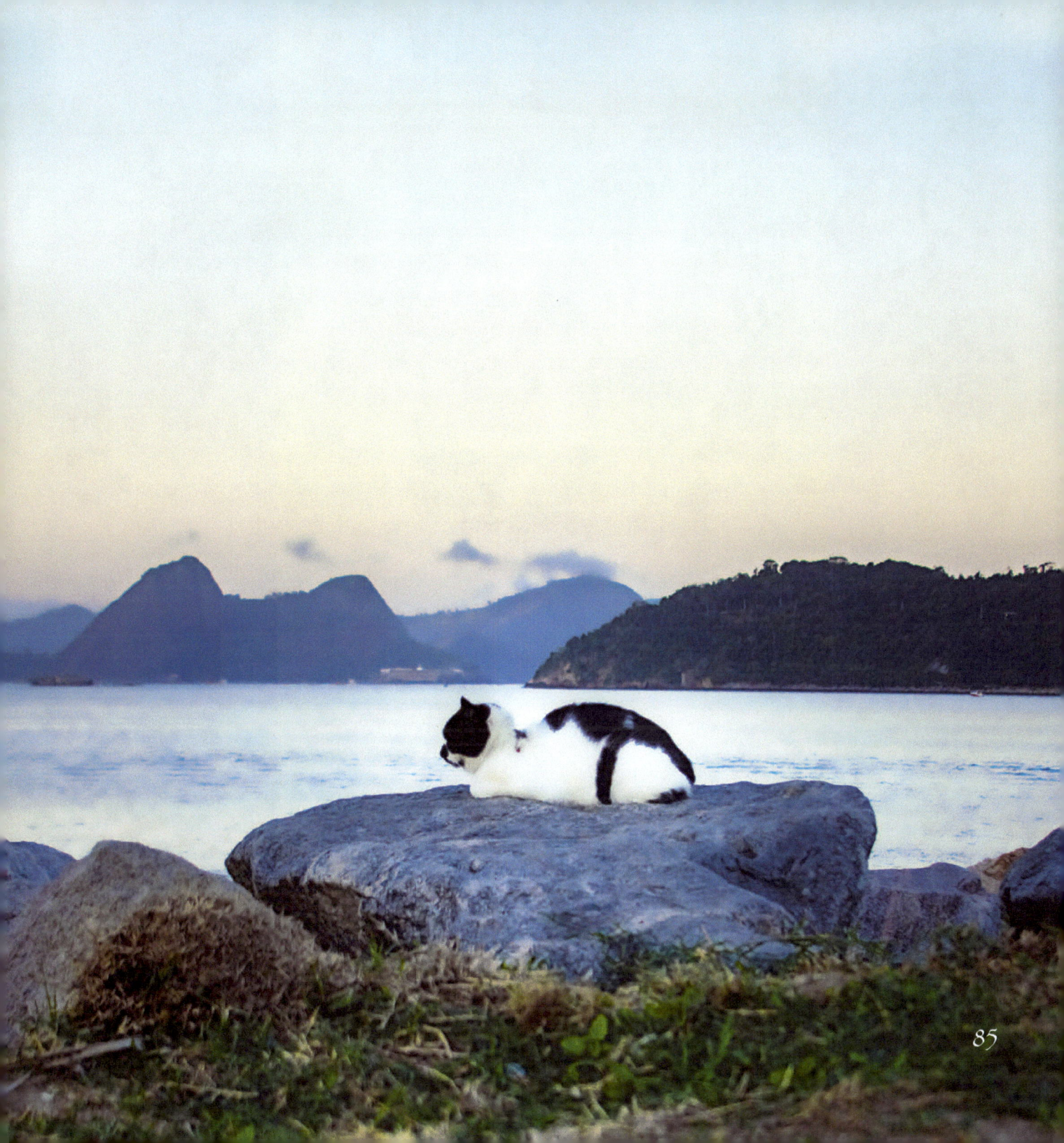

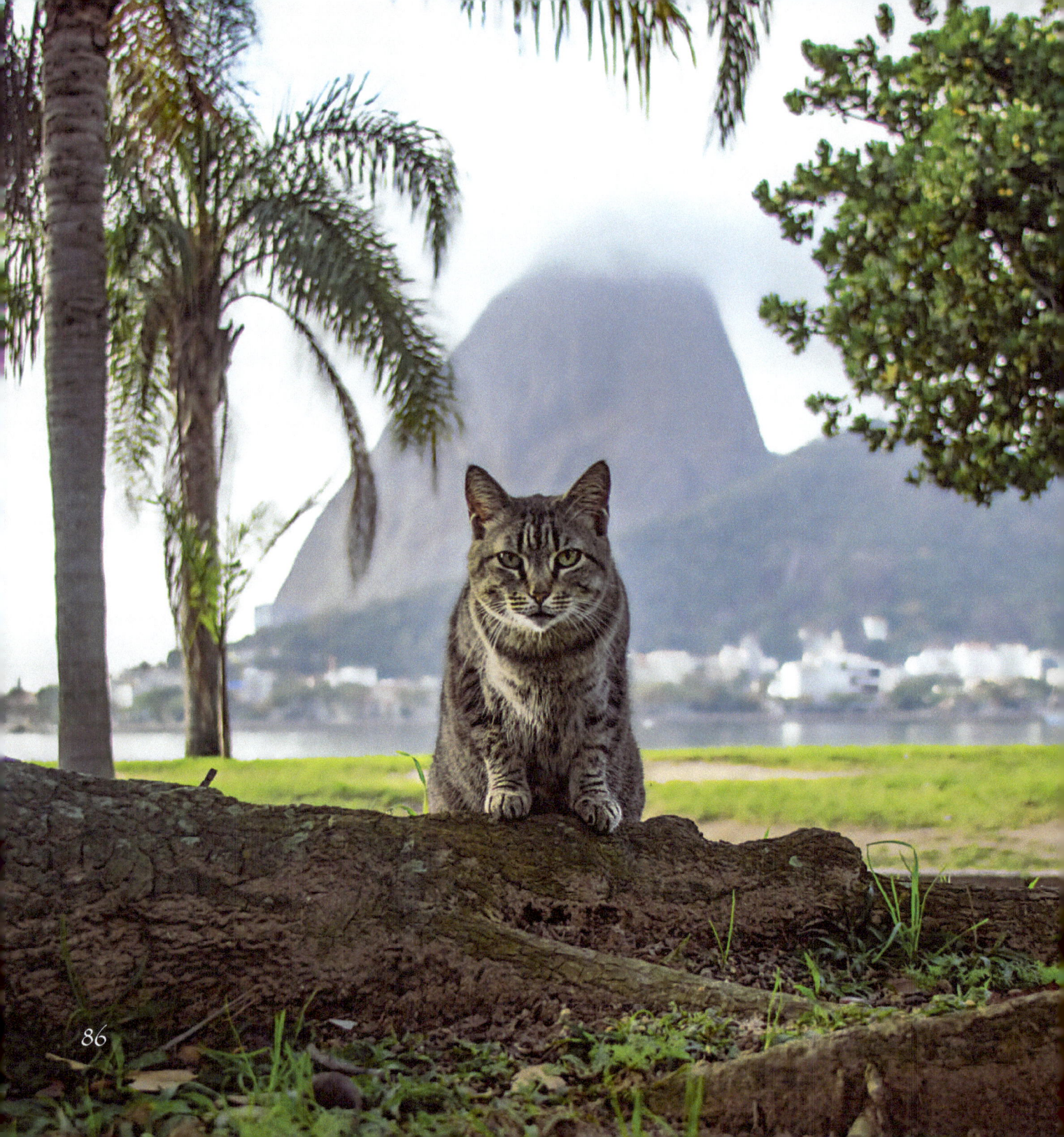

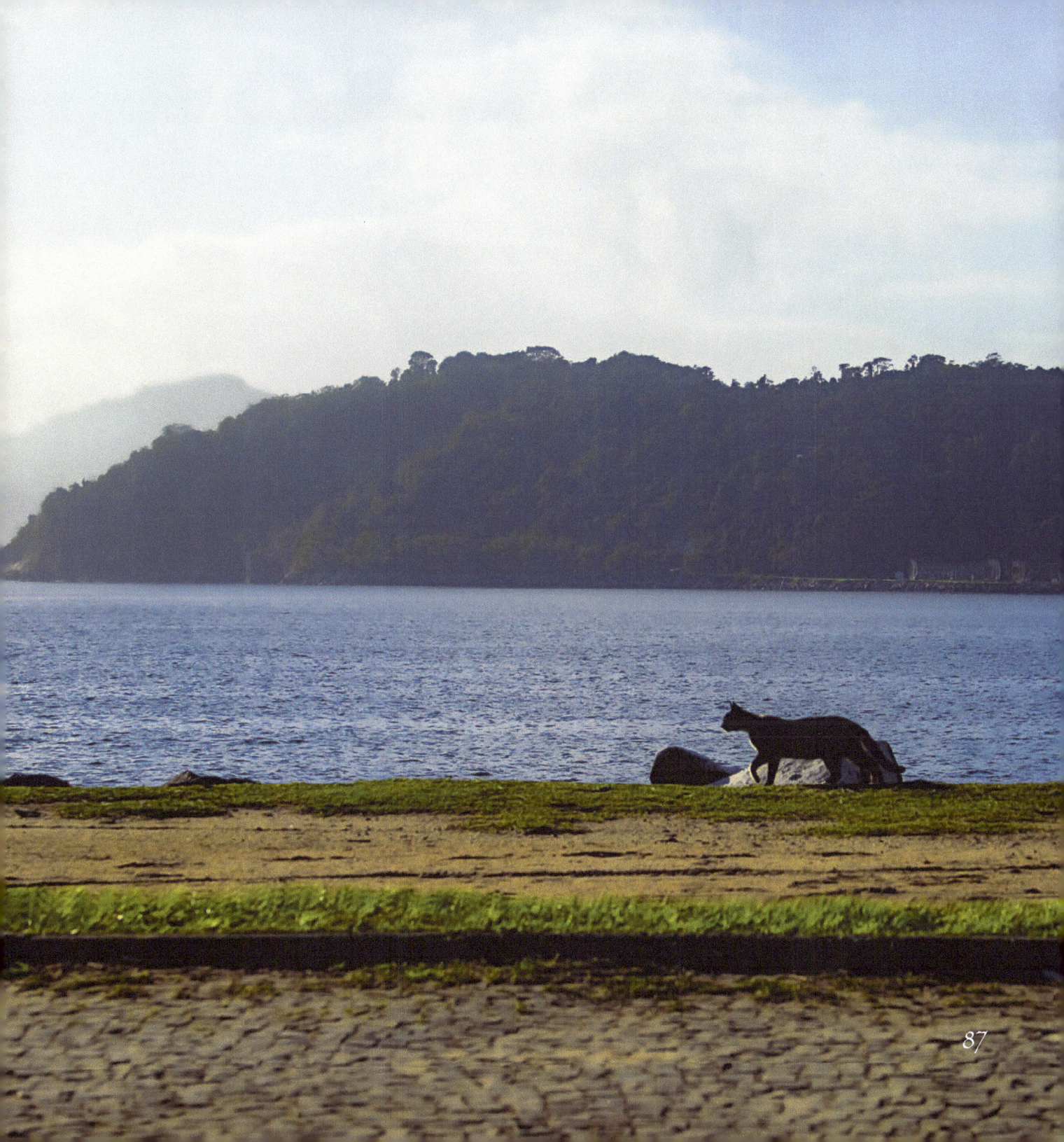

An adult cat have 30 teeth, 16 on the top and 14 on the bottom

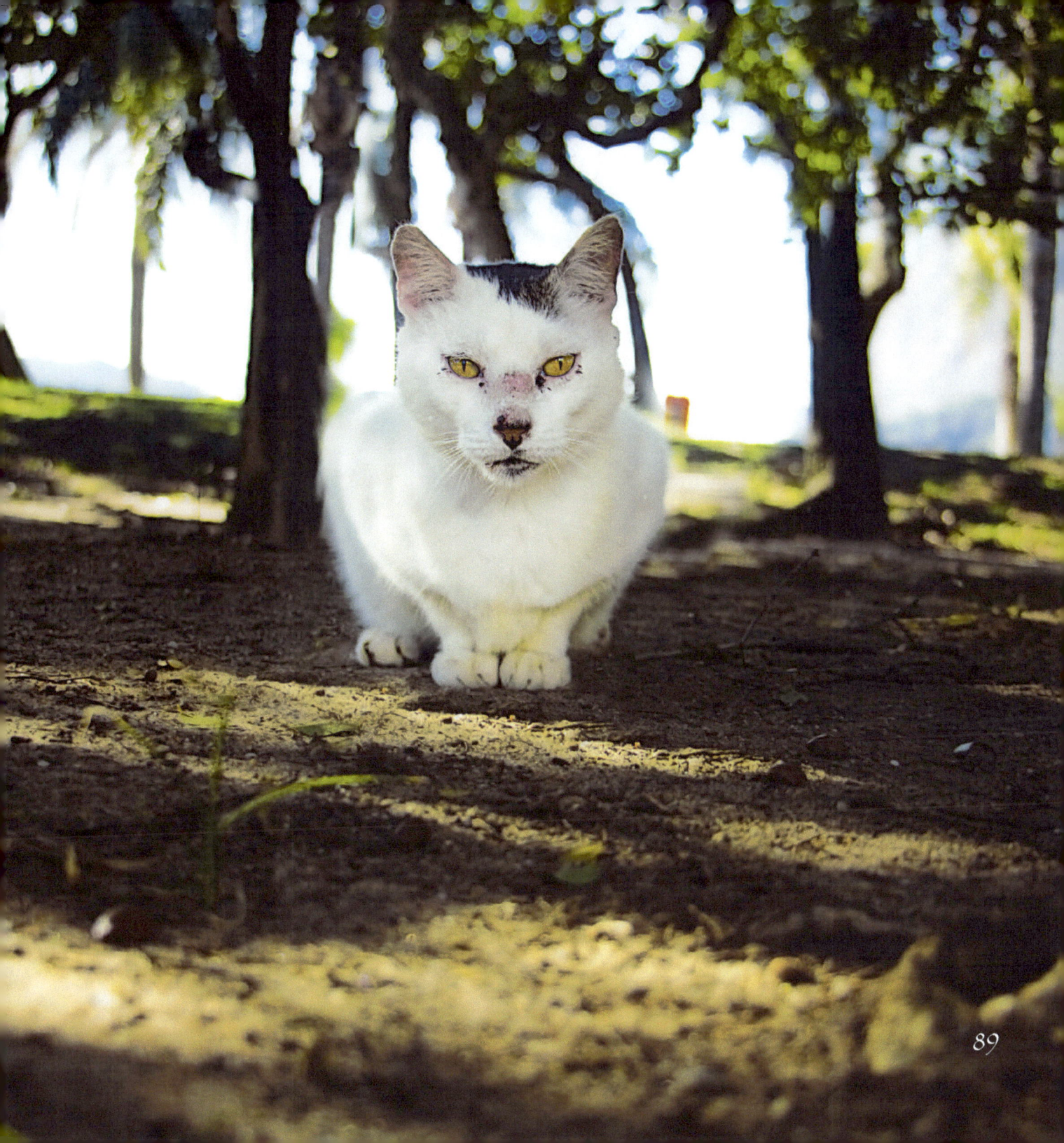

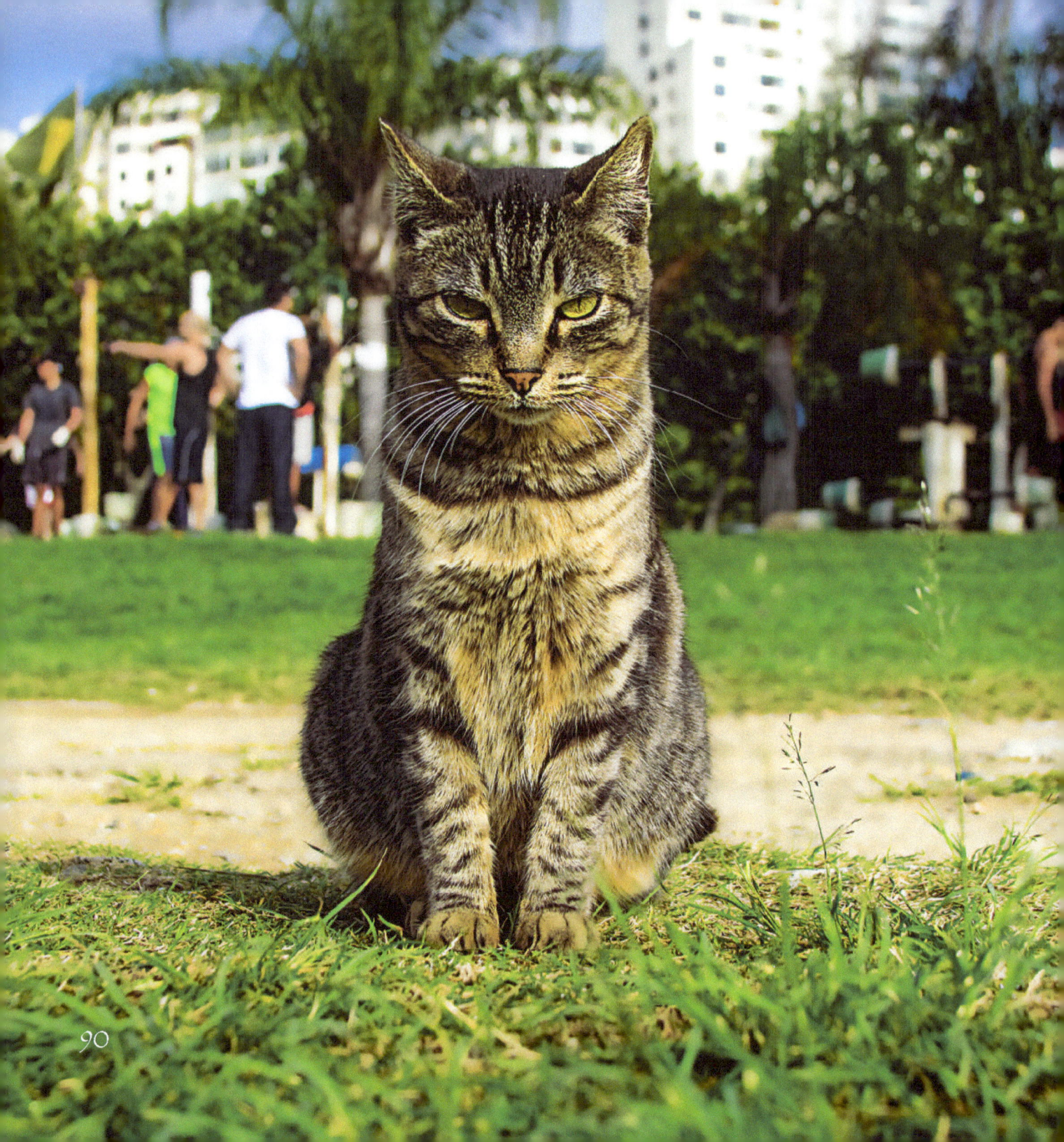

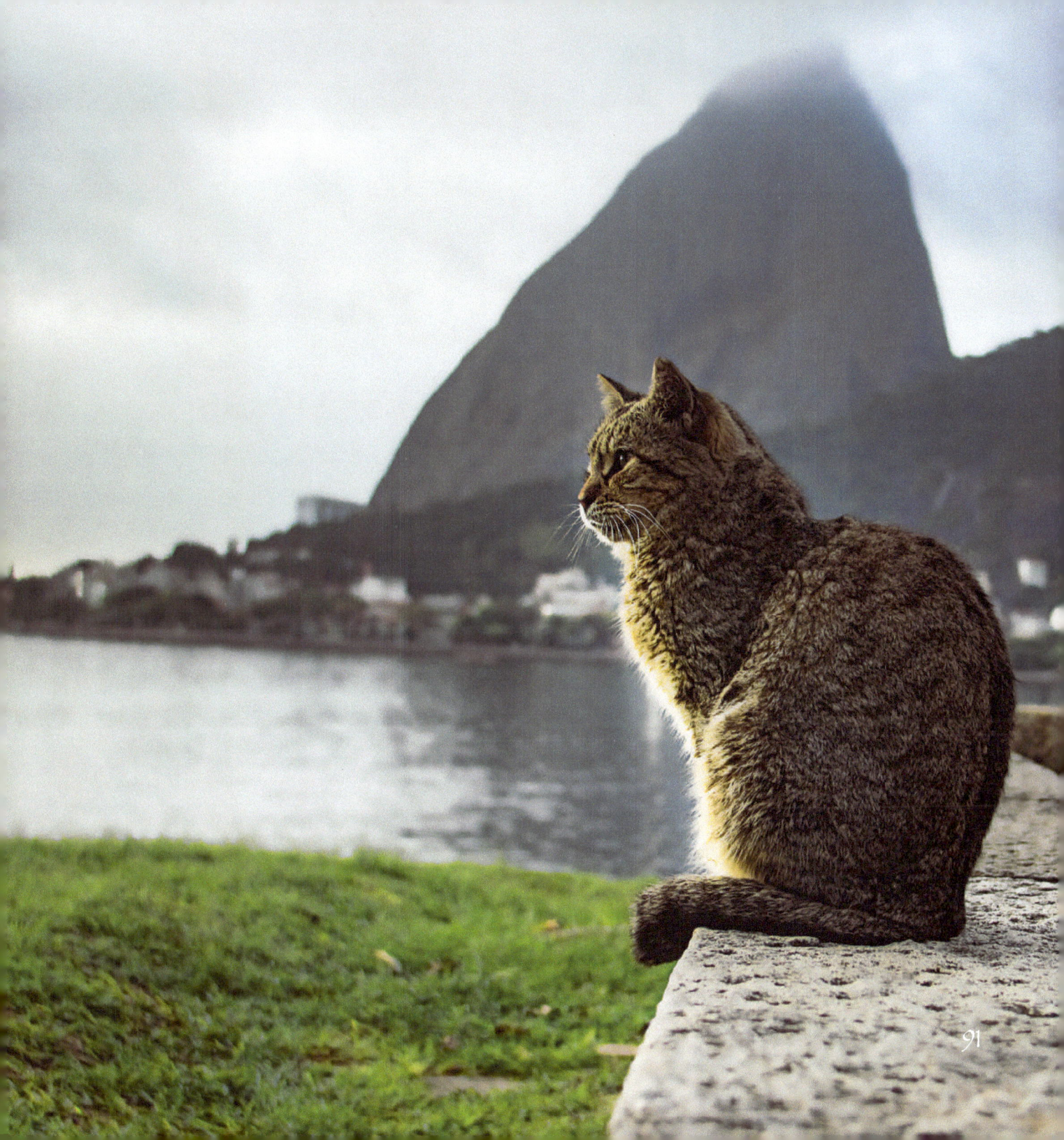

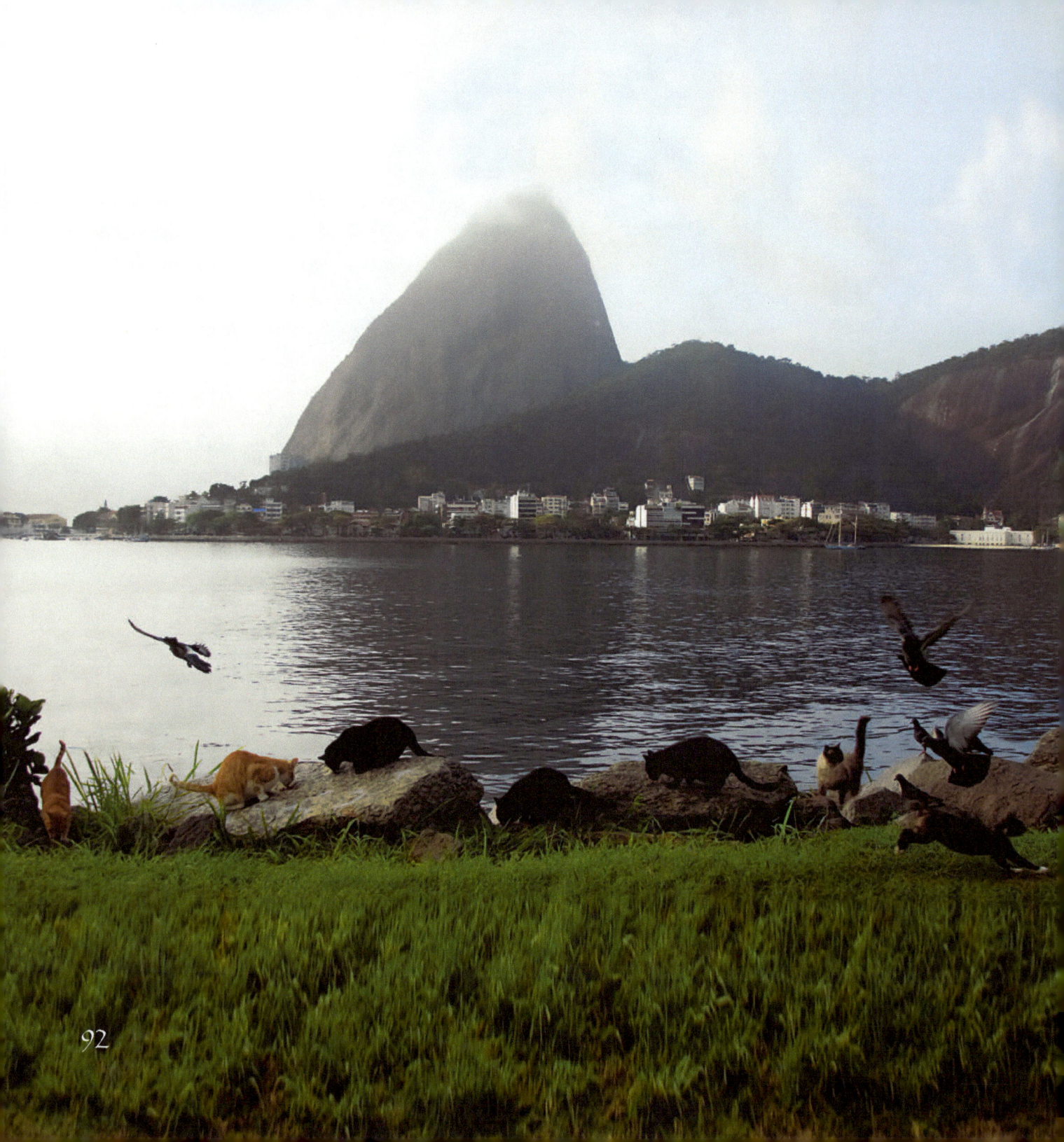

Portuguese is the official language of Brazil and it is the only
country in South America that speaks Portuguese

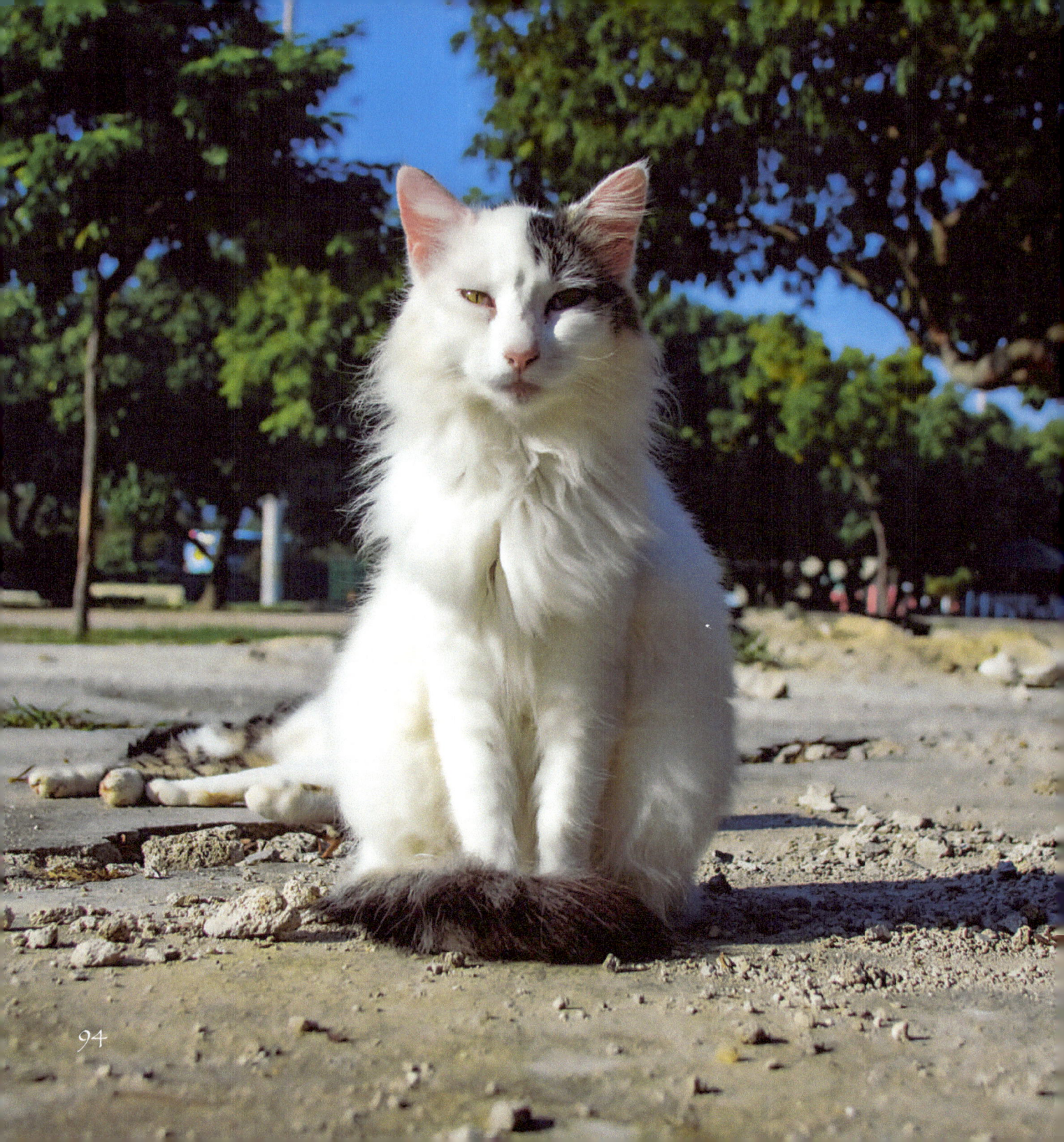

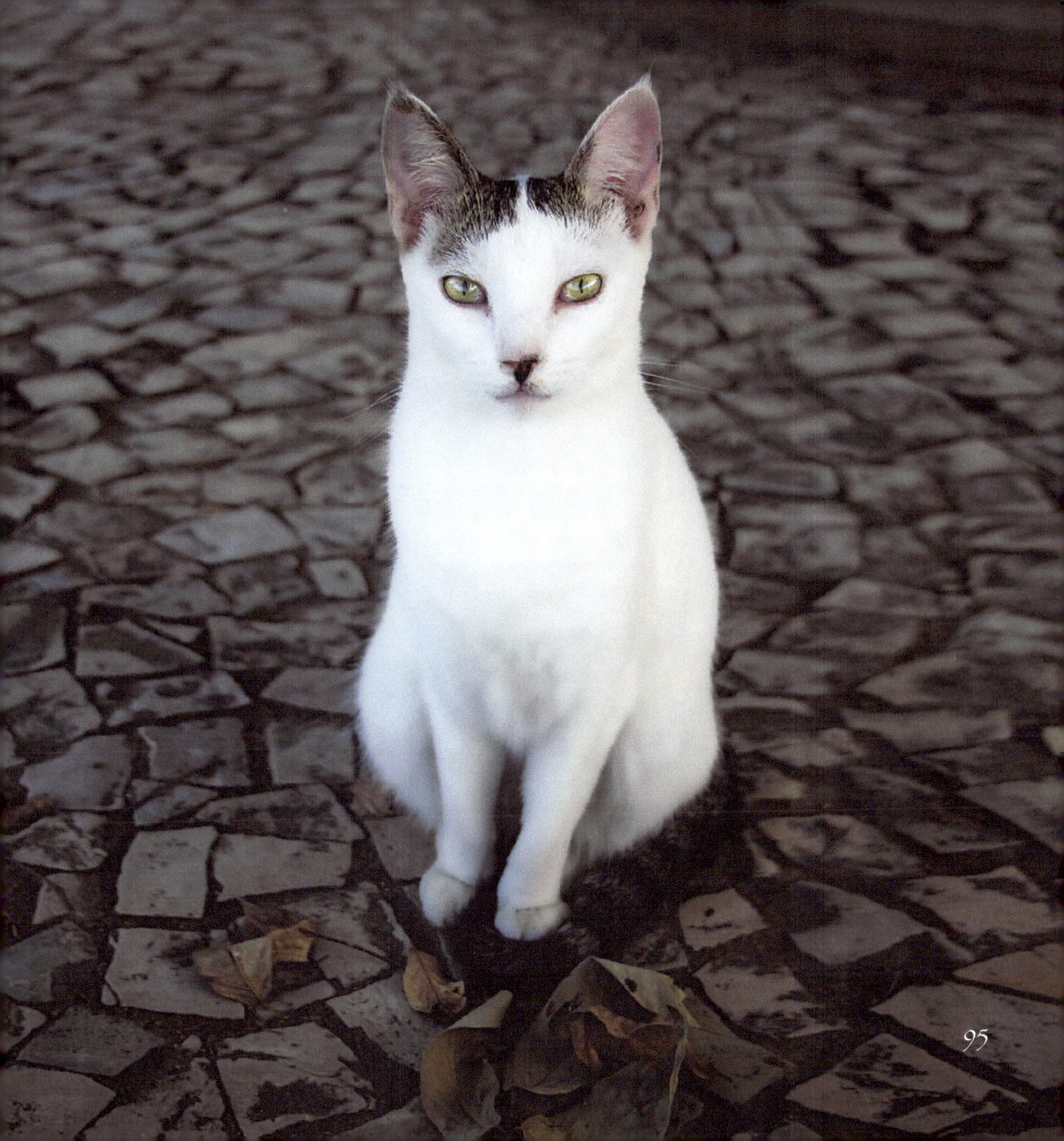

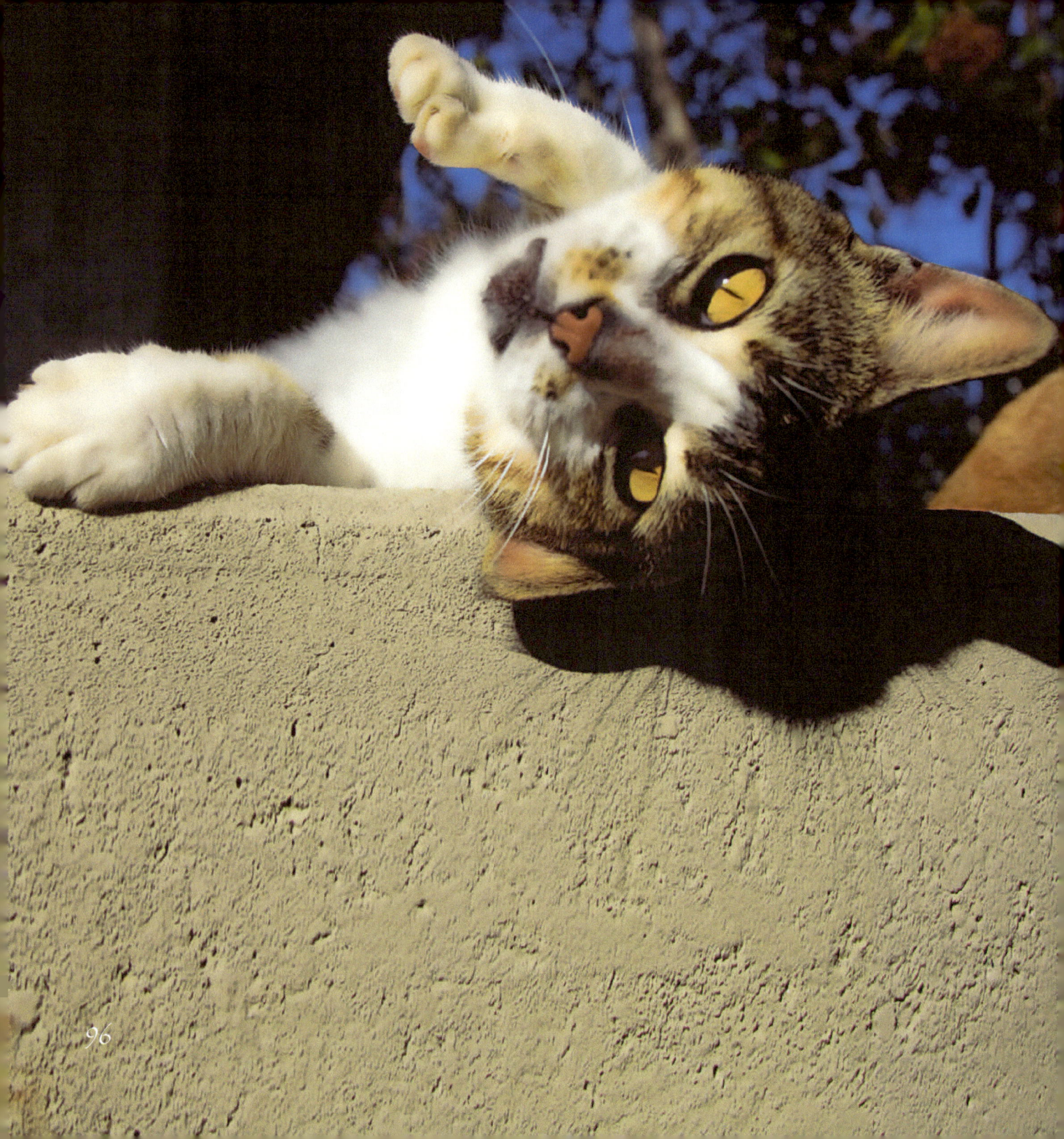

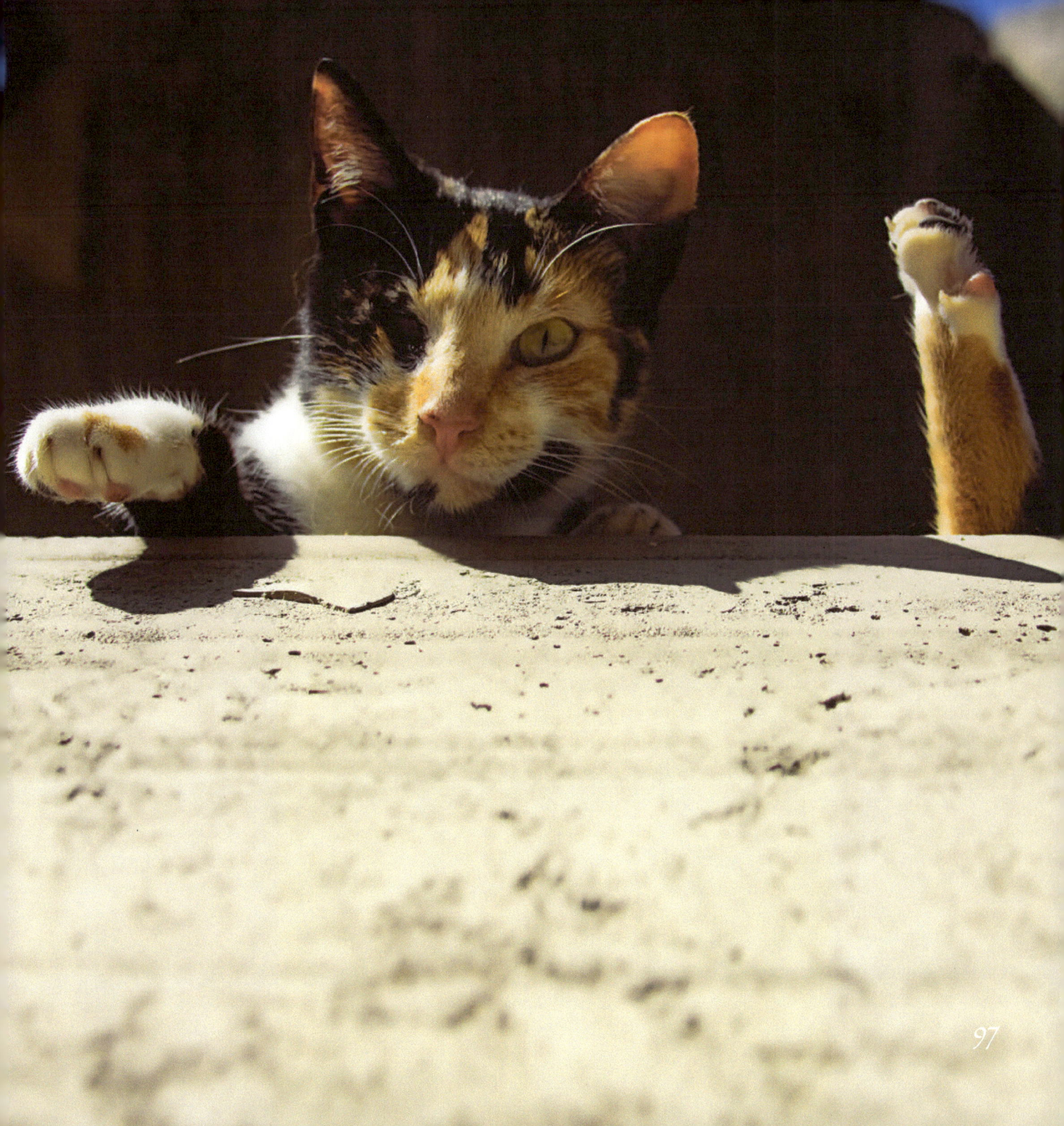

A domestic cat can run at speeds of 30 mph

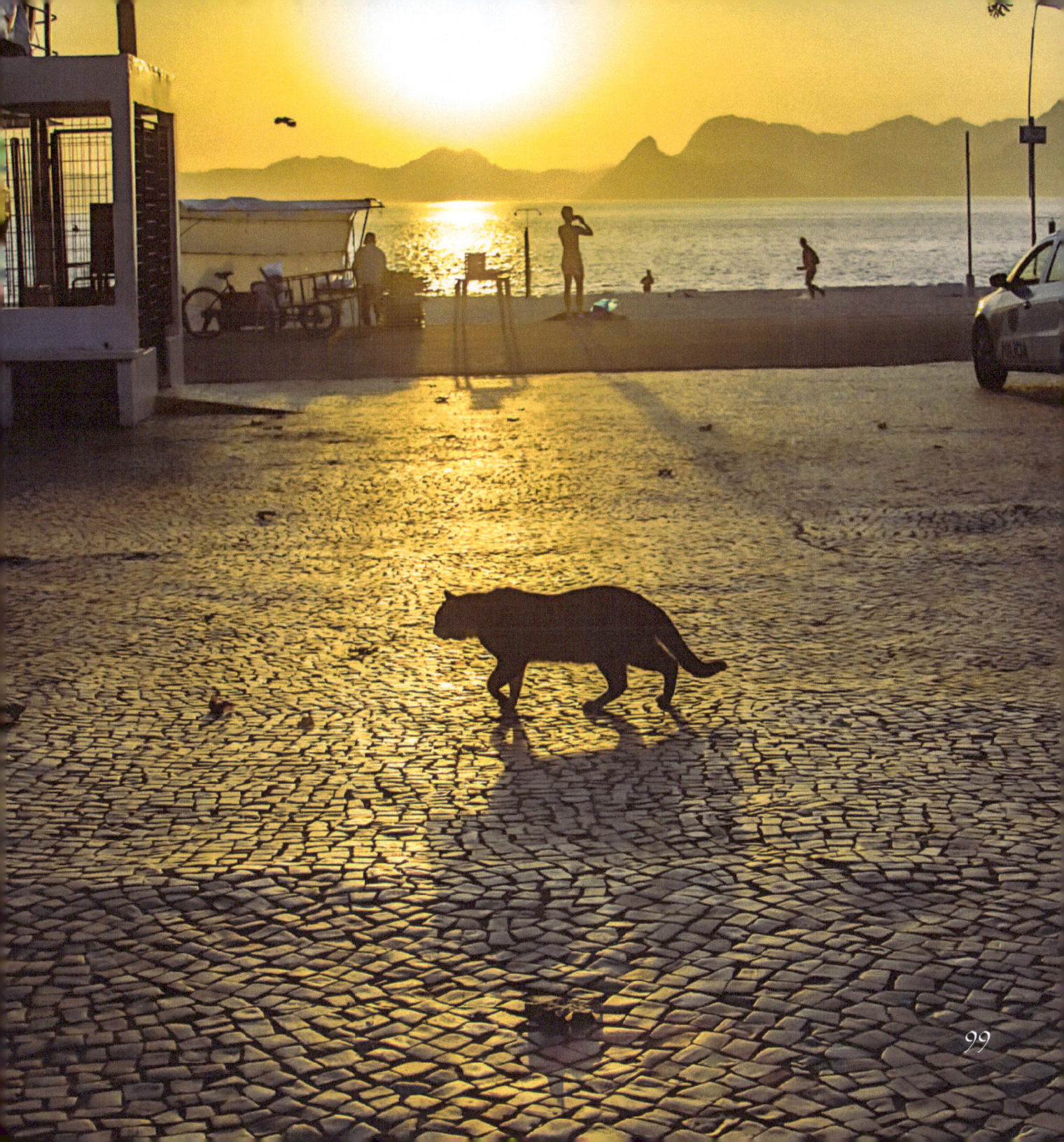

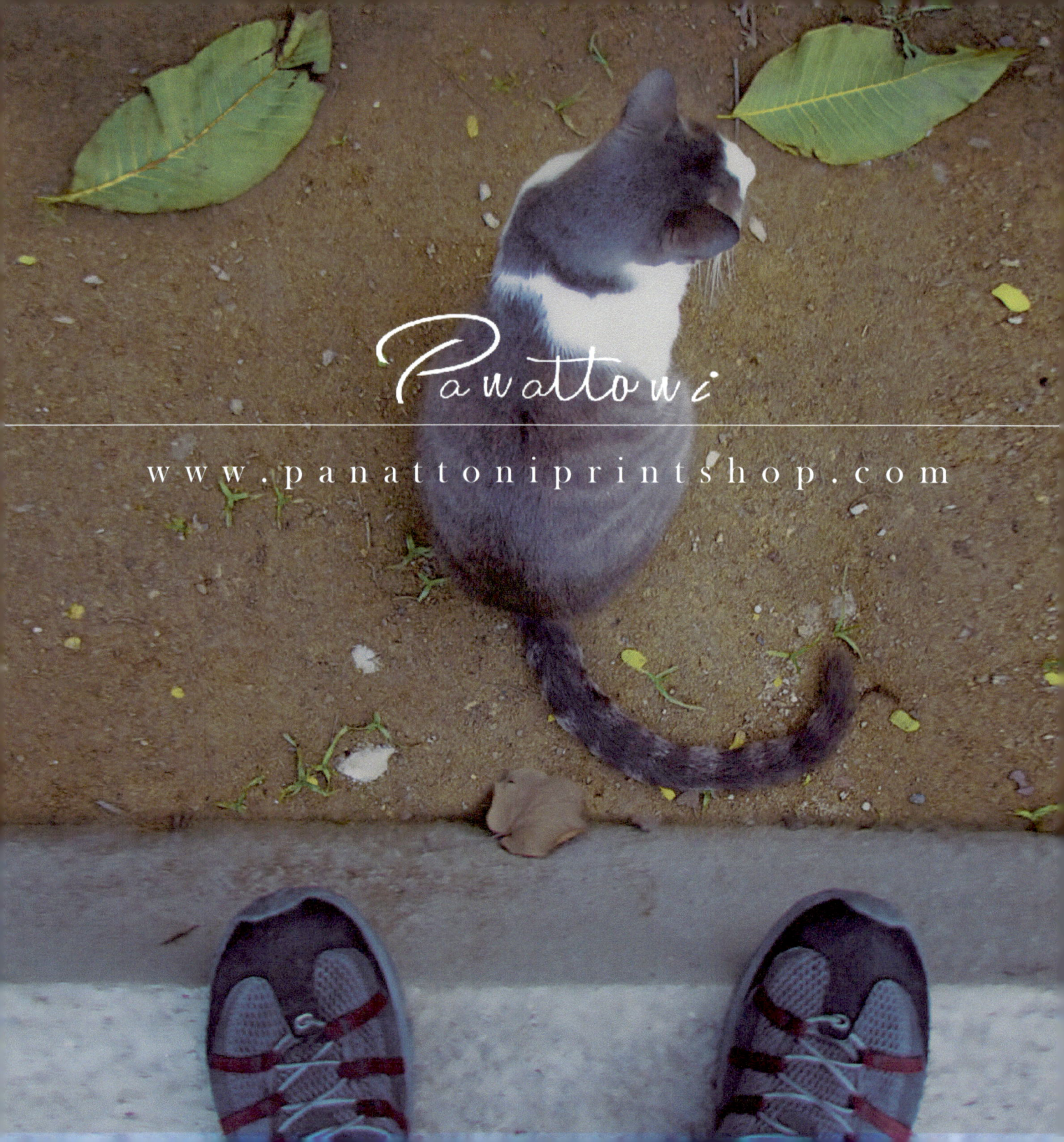

Panattoni

www.panattoniprintshop.com

www.ingramcontent.com/pod-product-compliance
Lightning Source LLC
Chambersburg PA
CBHW040323190526
45162CB00007B/58